KNOW YOUR REAL ENEMY

KNOW YOUR REAL ENEMY

MICHAEL YOUSSEF, PH.D.

A
JANET
THOMA
BOOK

THOMAS NELSON PUBLISHERS
Nashville • Atlanta • London • Vancouver

Published in Nashville, Tennessee, by Thomas Nelson, Inc., Publishers, and distributed in Canada by Word Communications, Ltd., Richmond, British Columbia.

Unless otherwise noted, Scripture quotations are from THE NEW KING JAMES VERSION. Copyright © 1979, 1980, 1982, Thomas Nelson, Inc., Publishers.

Scripture quotations noted NIV are from the HOLY BIBLE: NEW INTERNATIONAL VERSION. Copyright © 1973, 1978, 1984 by International Bible Society. Used by permission of Zondervan Publishing House. All rights reserved.

Library of Congress Cataloging-in-Publication Data

Youssef, Michael.
    Know your real enemy / Michael Youssef.
       p. cm.
    Includes bibliographical references.
    ISBN 0-7852-7102-3 (hc)
    1. Devil. 2. Spiritual warfare. I. Title.
BT981.Y78   1997
235'.4—dc21

                                    97–17518
                                       CIP

Printed in the United States of America.

1 2 3 4 5 6 BVG 02 01 00 99 98 97

DEDICATION

To Hank and Margaret McCamish, in deep appreciation
for more than two decades of encouragement and support

DEDICATION

CONTENTS

CONTENTS

ACKNOWLEDGMENTS

It is with heartfelt gratitude that I make the following acknowledgments to a number of people who helped make this book a reality.

Alicia McBride helped transcribe this material. Brenda Williams handled the many details that go into finalizing a book. David Lee is a brilliant editor who never tried to change my words but enhanced them.

Rolf Zettersten, publisher of Thomas Nelson Publishers, had the vision for this book and encouraged me to publish. I thank my editor, Janet Thoma of Janet Thoma Books, for her perception into both theology and communications, which made this book what it is. Her understanding of what is needed for a complete product is second to none. Her selfless hours of work were far beyond the call of duty.

Finally, my deepest gratitude goes to my wife and best friend, Elizabeth, who read and reread the material in its various stages, giving me so many words of encouragement. Ultimately, I am thankful to the faithful members of The Church of the Apostles, Atlanta, Georgia. When they heard this original material in sermon format from the pulpit, they were not only appreciative of the challenge and warning, but many encouraged me to make it available to a wider audience, hence this book.

PART ONE

KNOW
THE
ENEMY

KNOW WHO IS YOUR REAL ENEMY?

HOWARD LOCKE struggled with sexual sin. He was vice-principal of a Bible college, his wife loved him, and hundreds of students were influenced by his teaching. But he could not resist the lustful glance, could not keep sexual fantasies out of his head.

Carnal desire had gripped him for so long that secretly he had accommodated it. Howard started to pretend it wasn't his fault. He blamed his upbringing. He blamed his psychological makeup. In effect he said, "I don't want to be like this, but what can I do? This is the way I am." Eventually he lost his position after someone saw him buy a copy of *Playboy* at a newsstand. Howard's ministry was ruined by his failure to overcome sin. He knew it. But he was power-less to stop himself.

Many Christians have had experiences like Howard's—not necessarily with sexual sin, but in some area of their behavior or personality that they just cannot seem to control. As a result they live second-class lives, dogged by ineffectiveness and guilt. They go around in circles. Typically, they blame their failures on other people, or upbringing, or circumstances, and they try to fight failure using psychological methods, as though sin could be solved with therapy. Does it work? Of course not. And for one simple reason. The _real_ enemy in sin is not the influence of temperament or other people. The real enemy is the devil.

The same goes for relationships. If you're married, think for a moment about that last tiff you had with your spouse. Probably you felt your partner was in the wrong and felt wounded by your partner's lack of sensitivity and care. At first, arguments like that do little damage because the hurt is more than offset by mutual love and commitment. But it may not stay that way. Have enough arguments and you will find the battle lines being drawn. You begin to anticipate conflict, and to see your partner as responsible for your grievances. Sooner or later one of you begins to think, _If only I could get away from this person, my life would be so much better._

But again, who is the _real_ enemy? Whose interests are _really_ served when husband and wife start to fight? Not those of the marriage partners, still less those of their children.

Only one person wins when marriages break down, and that is the devil. So much hangs on a marriage: the health and security of children, management of the household, effective witnessing, your example to others. All these things Satan can seize and disrupt if he destroys a marriage. That's why marriages are under so much pressure.

Your soul and your relationships lie at the heart of a cosmic conflict. They can be won for God or lost to the devil. So get your priorities straight. Forget your niggling disagreements with the pastor; forget the way your husband or wife fails to live up to your expectations; forget that other person in the church who constantly gets on your nerves. If you're a Christian, you're fighting the *invisible war.*

THE INVISIBLE WAR

Like all wars, the invisible war has its battlefields.

I stumbled onto such a battlefield while touring Scotland. It was a church in the center of a famous old university town just north of Edinburgh. Like many ancient churches in Scotland, this was an architectural masterpiece and steeped in history. The great Reformer John Knox had once graced its pulpit. Crosses on the street outside marked the sites where Christian believers had been burned at the stake for their faith. Glorious victories had been won here for the gospel. As I stepped inside I saw a candle burning on the altar, and a sparrow flitting about in the roof overhead.

"How many people worship here?" I asked my companion, who lived in the town.

He smiled sadly. "Have a guess," he said.

"Five hundred?" I ventured. By Scottish standards the building was large.

"Try again."

"Two hundred?"

He shook his head. "Come here at eleven next Sunday and you'll see six people in the pews."

"*Six?*"

"Six elderly ladies. Let me tell you the story behind it."

And this is the story he told me. Twenty years ago the minister and the organist had a falling-out. Neither one can remember now what caused their disagreement. But since that time neither one has spoken a single word to the other. On Sunday morning the minister arrives early and places a list of hymns on the organ. The organist plays them, then leaves by a different door. In twenty years nobody new has joined the church, and slowly the existing congregation has died off.

When I heard that story I was powerfully reminded of Paul's parting words to the Ephesians:

Therefore take heed to yourselves and to all the flock, among which the Holy Spirit has made you overseers, to shepherd the church of God which He purchased with

His own blood. For I know this, that after my departure savage wolves will come in among you, not sparing the flock. Also from among yourselves men will rise up, speaking perverse things, to draw away the disciples after themselves. (Acts 20:28–30)

In that Scottish church two of the most influential believers had become enemies. But of course neither one of them was the *real* enemy. They were members of the same army—the army of God—and theirs was a brawl within the platoon. And a very serious one it was. It had cost the church its membership and crippled God's mission to the unsaved. In the invisible war that church was vital territory lost to Satan. Never mind the beauty of the architecture. Never mind the candle, or the sparrow flitting around the rafters. When I stepped through those doors I might as well have been in Prague the day after the Nazi tanks rolled in or in Saigon the day after the Vietcong invaded. The sorry tale of broken relationships and unresolved bitterness hid a deeper, spiritual truth: that the church was now in Enemy hands.

It is not hard to find other examples of churches lost to the devil. Very seldom are they taken by direct attack. Satan is too clever for that; if believers see him coming, he knows he will be repulsed. So he fights an invisible war. He proceeds by stealth. He dresses up his wolves as sheep, so that experience and discernment are needed to identify them.

No congregation is safe. Take an active, vibrant church that seeks to win the lost and equip the saints. One or two individuals come into the church and start to introduce new ideas. They say things like, "We need to move in a different direction. We need to do some social service, some counseling." Gently, and with arguments so subtle it's hard to refute them, they move the whole congregation out of the will of God. As a result, the mix of the membership changes. The original detractors gather more detractors around them, and within a short period of time the church has become both dead and deadly.

This is undercover work. When those wolves come in they look like sheep, they bleat like sheep, and the sheep befriend them. But the wolves are agents of the Enemy. Whether they realize it or not, they are being used to weaken the church's defenses and destroy it.

So how do we begin to win the invisible war, to keep the wolves at bay?

KNOW YOUR ENEMY!

Archie Parrish, an ex-serviceman and friend of many years, taught me a vital lesson. Archie told me of his experiences in the Korean War. "When I got there, they handed me a brochure. Every American soldier received one of these. It was titled *Know Your Enemy*." That brochure, he said, contained everything American soldiers needed to know about the North Koreans. What were they like? How did they think? Where did they attack? What was their ultimate goal? Knowing the answers to such questions would decide whether you won or lost. Any soldier doing a tour of duty in Korea would read and reread that brochure until he could repeat it backward. Knowledge gave strategic advantage; ignorance was death.

Tragically, when it comes to the invisible war, Christians are big on ignorance. Probably not one in ten believers would identify Satan as the real Enemy, much less know how to fight him. The average Christian is oblivious to spiritual conflict. The average Christian does not possess that vital, life-saving information on how to overcome Satan and his demonic cohorts. Consequently, the Enemy uses even born-again, Spirit-filled believers as his emissaries to destroy the work of God.

Did you catch what I just said?

If not, read it again. *The Enemy uses believers.* That's exactly what happened to Howard Locke. It's exactly what happened between the minister and the organist at that old church in Scotland. And it's exactly what is happening in countless Christian marriages and other Christian relationships the length and breadth of America. Once the devil has a foothold in your life, he will use it. You fight in this invisible war, but the war is also fought *in you.*

You say, "How can the Enemy get into a believer and use him to destroy God's work?" Well, the invisible war is much the same as ordinary war. A soldier in the regular army can easily serve his enemy's purposes, through cowardice, ignorance, inattention, or lack of resolve. Think what you like about the rights and wrongs of Vietnam: There is no denying that one of the reasons America lost in Vietnam was the lack of resolve and commitment on the part of the government leadership to fight to win. Halfheartedness is more serious than retreating.

In a similar way, surrendering your life to the lordship of Jesus Christ is not the end of the story. It is a decisive step. By acknowledging that there is no way to salvation except through Jesus, you move from darkness into light. You change your destination from hell to heaven. But you are not yet finished with your journey. You are not yet sanctified. You are like a massive corporation in the aftermath of a takeover—under new ownership, with new objectives, but with many of the old management structures still in place. Salvation takes time to soak in.

I want you to imagine it this way: In your spiritual being you are like a house with many doors. Each of those doors opens onto your soul, and each one needs to be bolted securely to prevent illegal entry. And despite the fact that you have surrendered your life to the Lord Jesus Christ, not all of those doors are locked. If Satan comes up and gives the doors a push, sooner or later he will find one that swings open. Now he has a way into your soul. He has found your Achilles' heel.

In the Middle East, where I grew up, professional thieves, generally speaking, don't break and enter. They don't *break*, that is. They go around the houses and push on the doors to see if anyone has left his door unlocked, and only then do they go in to steal and rob and destroy. Satan is a gentleman thief. He does not break and enter. If he comes into your life, it is because you have invited him, because one or two of those doors are swinging on their hinges.

This is a subject I will return to in more detail. Be aware now, though, of the number of doors you may be leaving unlocked. Anger is a door. If the door of anger is left unbolted, Satan will enter your life and create havoc in your relationships. Bitterness is a door. Hatred is a door. Lying is a door. Rebellion is a door. Jealousy is a door. Sexual lust is a door. Greed is a door. False guilt is a door. Shame is a door. Attraction to horoscopes and fortune-telling and the occult is a door. Are you understanding me? These doors, if they are not checked and bolted every day, will give the Enemy access to your soul.

And there is another door—the door I want to deal with first. That door is *ignorance*. For the first step to defeating your Enemy is *knowing him*. Know your Enemy. Know how to defeat him before he eats you for lunch, because that's what he wants to do. Know his operational procedure. Know what he thinks. Know when he attacks, how he attacks, where he attacks. Give yourself to the task of intelligence gathering. Any army worth its name remains in a constant state of readiness, alert to its enemy's activities.

The army that is well informed can never be overwhelmed by a surprise attack.

All this exhortation to readiness may have you worried. Is our Enemy in the invisible war so stealthy and powerful that we are in constant danger of being overrun? The answer, of course, is no. For one thing, we need to take the long view, and remember that the outcome of this war is already decided. No matter how many battles the devil may win, in the end he is going to be vanquished. That means we are the only army in history to be guaranteed success before firing a single shot. Our setbacks against the devil may be painful and costly, but they do not determine the final outcome.

Therefore we should take care to build the right attitude. We are on the winning side. Victory is assured. You may be saying, "I am not afraid of the devil." And that's fine. But that is not the central issue. Far more important is *whether the devil is afraid of you*. What have you done lately to scare the devil? What victory have you scored to make him run for cover?

When the great evangelist George Whitefield came to New England, a prominent and blue-blooded Bostonian minister confronted him and said, "Mr. Whitefield, I'm very sorry you came to Boston." To which the evangelist replied, "So is the devil, sir, so is the devil." Great crowds flocked to hear Whitefield, and as a result of his preaching the boundaries of God's kingdom were significantly extended.

The devil fears his final defeat, which is why he hates to be reminded of it. I was told that an eminent preacher once explained why many Christians refuse to believe in the Bible as the authoritative Word of God. He said, "They call Genesis a myth and the Revelation a mystery." In his opinion, no man was clever enough to come up with objections like this—they sprang from the devil himself. "And the reason," he said, "why the devil is so anxious to get rid of Genesis and Revelation, is that in Genesis his sentence is declared, and in Revelation it is executed."

Let me give you some encouragement. Right now—right this very second—you have got the devil on the run. Why? Simply because you are taking the time and trouble to do what he most hates to see. You are getting to know your Enemy, uncovering his weaknesses, countering his strengths. For that reason, he will do his utmost to prevent you from finishing this book. And when you have finished it he will do his utmost to make you forget what it said. So why not make the devil really mad? Go get a notepad and pen, and start writing down what the Spirit of God is teaching you.

In the chapters that follow we will look at a number of crucial and difficult areas. We will learn about the devil's command structures and strategies, his preferred methods of attack, and his ultimate destruction. Before that, though, I want to sketch in some of the background and ask what many people consider to be the biggest question of all: Where did the devil come from?

WHERE DID THE DEVIL COME FROM?

Turn with me to two key biblical passages: Ezekiel 28:11–19, and Isaiah 14:12–15—passages in which we find the most definitive biblical teaching on the origin of Satan.

In these passages neither Ezekiel nor Isaiah addressed Satan directly. Instead their taunts were directed against contemporary leaders whose opposition to God made them *types* of Satan. God instructed Ezekiel: "Son of man, take up a lamentation for the king of Tyre" (Ezek. 28:12a). Similarly, Isaiah was told to "take up this proverb against the king of Babylon" (Isa. 14:4). All the enemies of God in the Old Testament were types of Satan, including the pharaoh confronted by Moses. And wherever these types are found, we can be sure the Bible is teaching us something important about the devil. Even today any king, any prince, any president, or any ruler who refuses or rejects God acts in effect as Satan's personal representative. Any government that rejects God becomes the seat of Satan. Why? Because Satan uses people to accomplish his purpose. Satan always employs willing agents to do his evil bidding.

The first clue to Satan's origins is found in Isaiah's use of the name *Lucifer:*

> *How you are fallen from heaven,*
> *O Lucifer, son of the morning!*

How you are cut down to the ground,
You who weakened the nations! (Isa. 14:12)

At first this seems paradoxical. The name *Lucifer* literally means *light-bearer, the brilliant one, the shining one.* Ezekiel affirmed this same truth by picturing Satan dressed in a sort of glitter-suit of precious stones. God said of him:

You were the seal of perfection,
Full of wisdom and perfect in beauty.
You were in Eden, the garden of God;
Every precious stone was your covering:
The sardius, topaz, and diamond,
Beryl, onyx, and jasper,
Sapphire, turquoise, and emerald with gold.
(Ezek. 28:12b–13a)

In contrast to Ezekiel, Paul later described the Ephesians' struggle against "the rulers of the darkness of this age, against spiritual hosts of wickedness in the heavenly places" (Eph. 6:12b). How can Satan's realm of darkness be presided over by one who was called the bearer of light?

Remember, we are talking about *origins* here. God created Lucifer to be one of his principal servants. Read further in Ezekiel:

You were the anointed cherub who covers;
I established you;

You were on the holy mountain of God;
You walked back and forth in the midst of fiery stones.
You were perfect in your ways from the day you were
  created,
Till iniquity was found in you. (28:14–15)

According to Ezekiel, Satan was "the seal of perfection, / Full of wisdom and perfect in beauty." Even so, Lucifer's light was the light of a mirror, not that of a torch. The light never originated within him. Not one of those precious stones described in Ezekiel 28 could shine by itself; put it in a dark room and you wouldn't even see it. Lucifer shone because he *reflected* the beauty and light of God. Don't forget that Lucifer was one of the most senior angels. He worked at the highest level. Unlike Moses, who had to cover his face in the presence of God, Lucifer was able to look at God's very throne. He was able to voice praise, to voice adoration, to voice worship to God. Such was his privilege, and the authority he had from on high.

Incidentally, this is what makes Satan such a cunning and dangerous adversary. He is like a top-ranking defector from the CIA, who knows the protocols and the secret codes, who can pick up his old contacts and be absolutely convincing. For this reason Paul wrote to the Corinthians:

For such are false apostles, deceitful workers, transform-
ing themselves into apostles of Christ. And no wonder!

For Satan himself transforms himself into an angel of light. (2 Cor. 11:13–14)

Satan knows exactly how to look like an angel of light, because that is what he was. That is what God created him to be: Lucifer. Not because he had any beauty of his own, but because he would so magnificently reflect the beauty and glory of his Creator. And don't miss what Paul wrote about those false apostles "transforming themselves into apostles of Christ." The wolves take after their leader; they are masters of disguise. In a later chapter I will return to this problem and show how effectively, even now, Satan's cohorts are being sent to masquerade as true believers.

Pride Came Before the Fall

But let's look at a second clue to Satan's origins. He was created by the one true eternal God, who has no beginning and no end. As a created being he was obliged to offer worship, to offer praise, to adore the Creator God. He was perfect in every way. He was the epitome of wisdom. He was the ultimate in beauty. But he was created for a purpose. God delegated to him full executive responsibility for the angelic hosts who serve him throughout the universe.

The Bible does not tell us how many there are in this host. *Zillions*, today's kids would say. But even zillions seems an underestimate. And within this heavenly host, Paul tells us in Ephesians 1:21, there are numerous ranks, classes, and grades. Each rank or class or grade has a different responsibility. Each has a different area of ministry. Each has a sphere of work that is different from the others. Read Revelation and you will find that the job of some angels is to stand constantly before the throne of God, saying "Holy, holy, holy, / Lord God Almighty, / who was and is and is to come." The only thing the Bible says of *all* angels—in Hebrews 1:14—is that they are "ministering spirits."

It seems that Lucifer presided over this entire group. He was the executive assistant. And this position brought him an awesome power. He acted as top intermediary, chief middleman. He gathered worship from every part of creation and brought it into the presence of God. But being a middleman, even chief middleman, isn't easy. It requires supernatural humility, and supernatural maturity. Ask any top executive. Sure, you know how far you have risen and how many people are down there below you. But the closer you get to the top, the more intensely you desire to climb that final rung and become the undisputed head. In corporate life, perhaps, this is not such an unreasonable ambition; the move from executive assistant to CEO is not such a large one. But an unbridgeable gulf separates creature from Creator; consequently, for Lucifer to entertain the ambition of replacing God was not only blasphemous but irrational.

An insight into Lucifer's thought processes at this point was given by Isaiah:

For you have said in your heart:
"I will ascend into heaven,
I will exalt my throne above the stars of God;
I will also sit on the mount of the congregation
On the farthest sides of the north;
I will ascend above the heights of the clouds,
I will be like the Most High." (Isa. 14:13–14)

See the verbs by which Lucifer expressed his ambition: "I will ascend . . . I will exalt my throne . . . I will also sit . . . I will ascend above . . . I will be like . . ." Five times in two verses the same words appear: *I will.* God created Lucifer perfect, but he also created him with the capacity to choose—just as he did Adam and Eve. To have the power of choice is to be, in a special way, aware of yourself as the chooser. It opens the possibility of becoming so focused on yourself that you forget how insignificant you really are. Holding up your hand in front of your face, you believe your hand to be larger than a mountain on the horizon. You begin to equate yourself with God. And from this fatal perceptual error spring all kinds of evil: self-concern, pride, and false ambition.

This is what happened to Lucifer. He became proud of his beauty. He became proud of his intellect. He became proud of his capacity. He became proud of his attainment. He failed to recognize that everything he possessed was a gift from God, and that without God he was nothing. He really thought he deserved worship in his own right.

Ezekiel put it well when he said to Satan, "Your heart was lifted up because of your beauty; / You corrupted your wisdom for the sake of your splendor" (Ezek. 28:17a).

And that is why God fired him and threw him out of heaven. Jesus referred to this event when he said, "I saw Satan fall like lightning from heaven" (Luke 10:18). Here is Ezekiel's version:

> *Therefore I cast you as a profane thing*
> *Out of the mountain of God;*
> *And I destroyed you, O covering cherub,*
> *From the midst of the fiery stones. . . .*
> *I cast you to the ground,*
> *I laid you before kings,*
> *That they might gaze at you.* (Ezek. 28:16b, 17b)

THREE QUESTIONS AND A WARNING

At this point some Christians find fault with God. Didn't God know from the beginning, they ask, that pride would capture the heart of Lucifer? The answer is yes, because God is omniscient, and being omniscient means you know everything ahead of time. So, could God not have prevented Satan's fall? Again the answer is yes, because God is also omnipotent. He can do anything. And here comes the third question. If God knew Lucifer would rebel, and if God could have prevented it, why didn't he do so?

Well, why didn't he? On the face of it, preventing Satan's rebellion would have saved an awful lot of trouble. There would have been no fall in Eden, no history of human sin, no need for redemption, no destruction of the present order to make way for the new heavens and new earth. The closest we can get to answering this question is to point to the importance of free will. Without free will, after all, created beings are only machines. Like computers, they do exactly what they are told to do—no more, no less. It could be argued that we are only real persons at all to the extent that we are free—free even to reject God. Here, though, we are moving out of the circle of biblical certainty and into the realm of speculation.

At this point there is a far more pressing issue to consider. If you forget everything else I've said so far, don't forget what I'm going to say now.

Lucifer's sin has been reproduced again and again throughout history. It was reproduced in Adam and Eve when they believed the serpent's lie and wanted to be like God. It was reproduced when the people of Israel arrived in the promised land, only to turn their backs on God and worship Baal. It was reproduced again when the proud Pharisees refused to repent and believe in the Lord Jesus Christ, the real light of God, the only anointed Messiah, and the only Savior. It is repeated every single day when an unsaved person refuses to submit to the authority of God's Son. Lucifer's sin is reproduced again and again. For the unsaved do not want to acknowledge that they cannot

KNOW YOUR REAL ENEMY

know God by their own minds, that they cannot reach God by their good works, that they cannot be saved their own way.

But worse than that, Satan's sin is also being reproduced among believers. This is why the apostle Paul warned Timothy not to let an immature Christian assume a position of leadership. This is not reverse ageism. Paul was not talking about physical maturity, but spiritual maturity. How many Christian leaders have we seen in America in the last twenty years who have been disgraced through their immaturity? Such a person, said Paul, should be kept from leadership responsibility "lest being puffed up with pride he fall into the same condemnation as the devil" (1 Tim. 3:6).

So be warned, whoever you are—man or woman, clergy or layperson, adult or child. You are never closer to Satan, or more clearly under Satan's control, than when pride drives you. Pride distorts your judgment. It makes you covet things you have no right to. It alienates you from God. No temptation confronts us more persistently or entices us more subtly than the temptation of pride, because through pride Satan reproduces himself. So let no one "think of himself more highly than he ought" (Rom. 12:3)—for to do so is to think as the Enemy thinks.

As you learn about the Enemy, examine yourself for traces of pride—pride of knowledge, pride of achievement, pride of position, pride of possession, even pride in your cleverness at thwarting Satan. Whatever form it takes, pride will always bring you to the doors of the recruiting office where the devil turns sheep into wolves.

Don't let it happen to you.

KNOW THE ENEMY: YOUR A REAL SEVEN-POINT ENEMY PROFILE

A MAN WENT to his doctor for a thorough physical examination. Afterward he said, "Doctor, give it to me straight. I can take it. Just tell me what's wrong with me."

The doctor said, "Do you really want to know?"

"Oh, yes," replied the man, "Don't dress it up in fancy language. I want the truth in plain English. What's really wrong with me?"

"Well," the doctor said, "there is really nothing wrong with you, except that you're lazy."

The man thought for a minute and said, "Okay, now give me the medical term so I can tell my wife."

In spite of the man's claim to want the truth in plain English, he wanted to deceive his wife into believing he had a medical condition. *Deception* is one of your Enemy's chief weapons. For instance, see how the book of Revelation describes his fall from heaven:

> *So the great dragon was cast out, that serpent of old, called the Devil and Satan, who deceives the whole world; he was cast to the earth, and his angels were cast out with him.* (Rev. 12:9)

The devil *deceives the whole world.* Now think about that. It is quite a feat. Not even the most wily politician could manage it. How does the Enemy succeed? One thing we can see immediately is that Satan, like the perfect salesperson, believes wholeheartedly in his own product. We discovered in the last chapter that Satan thinks he *deserves* the worship due to God. In fact, he has fallen for his own PR. Before deceiving anyone else, he has completely deceived himself. He really believes the falsehoods he peddles to others.

This means we should never expect the Enemy to come clean about deception. He is never going to tap you on the shoulder and say, "Now Mr. So-and-so, now Miss So-and-so, my name is the devil and today I'm going to deceive you." What would be the point? He is too clever for that. Ninety-nine times out of a hundred you will not even know it's the devil who is tempting you, and it will not even occur to you that you're being tempted.

Sadly, experience in leadership does not always make you resistant to deceit. Over the years too many prominent Christians have shown themselves naive in the face of temptation. That, in short, is why so many mainline churches and so many once-godly schools have strayed from the intentions of their founders. Successive leaders have unwittingly listened to the voice of Satan and taken the institutions entrusted to their care straight into a blind alley. Actually, this should not surprise us. The Enemy targets Christian leaders, and his purposes are often doggedly pursued by ordained ministers, elders of the church, heads of schools, and presidents of colleges. Leaders are as vulnerable to deception as anyone else. Perceiving the Enemy's assaults, and countering them, takes a special kind of gift.

Paul had this gift. Paul wrote of the Enemy: "We are not ignorant of his devices" (2 Cor. 2:11b). The apostle Paul had the same instinctive grasp of Satan's methods as a seasoned detective might have of the criminal mind. He understood Satan's philosophy. He understood his character. He understood his purpose. He understood his method of operation.

So what traits characterize the Enemy? How can we recognize him? We need to know that for as long as his disguise remains intact, the Enemy will move among us undetected and unchallenged. He will surprise and ambush us, and inch by inch, soul by soul, relationship by relationship, church by church, invade God's territory in the invisible war.

KNOW YOUR REAL ENEMY

In this chapter, then, I want to look at seven facts about the devil. Together they give us an essential profile. Armed with this profile we will know whom we're looking for, we will have a description of him, and we will no longer be fighting a phantom. As you study the Enemy and build up his profile, evaluate yourself for signs of the devil's work in your own life. Have you in any way begun to model your lifestyle on the deceptions of the devil instead of the truths of God? Do you imitate the Enemy of God, or do you endeavor to imitate the Savior of your soul? Do you deceive, slander, and malign, or do you encourage, uplift, and uphold? Read carefully, and think hard.

Fact #1: The Enemy Believes in Questioning Authority

Growing up in Egypt I heard many stories about the Battle of El Alamein, fought during the Second World War on Egyptian soil.

In 1942 the Allies found themselves unable to achieve a decisive victory against Rommel in the Egyptian western desert. Rommel had been nicknamed the Desert Fox, because he had so often and so effectively outmaneuvered the Allied forces. Finally, fearing Rommel would outwit them, Churchill sent in Field Marshall Bernard Montgomery to take the Allied command.

Montgomery was an autocratic and persistent general. Churchill called him "indomitable in retreat, invincible in advance, insufferable in victory." He was the man who finally outfoxed the Desert Fox and won the Battle of El Alamein. But how did he do it? The answer is surprisingly simple. Montgomery discovered that under the previous leadership almost every order had been questioned by subordinate officers, all the way down to the lowest ranks. In effect, the Allies had been paralyzed by disagreement. Montgomery immediately put a stop to it. Under his leadership orders were not questioned, debated, or discussed—they were simply obeyed. And in that lay the secret of victory.

A similar questioning of orders lays at the heart of the devil's fall. He questioned the authority of God. And now that he has been thrown out of heaven he likes nothing better than to see others doing the same thing. He wants Christians to be paralyzed, just as the Allied forces were in the war with Rommel—by persistently having them turn a *command* into a *debate*.

If you doubt that, go back to the beginning. Leaf through the opening pages of your Bible and see what happened in the first encounter between humankind and the devil. In particular, look at Genesis 3:1–7, the conversation between the serpent and Eve. We often make the mistake of assuming that Adam and Eve were pushovers. It's not true. Adam and Eve lived in closer communion with God than any of us do today. To topple them, Satan would need to use all his craftiness. How did he do it?

Satan, the serpent, did not confront Eve with the straight truth. He did not say, "Eve, if you obey me instead of God, you and all my fallen angels will wind up in the lake of fire, which has been prepared for us." Nor did he accuse God bluntly of lying. Instead, he led with a *question:*

Now the serpent was more cunning than any beast of the field which the LORD God had made. And he said to the woman, "Has God indeed said, 'You shall not eat of every tree of the garden'?" (Gen. 3:1)

Notice that he turned the command into a debate. In effect he said, "Eve, did God really say it that way? Did you hear it right? Did you really understand him correctly?" Without making any false allegations, he made it possible for Eve to debate the truth of God's word. Notice something else too. The New King James Version describes the serpent as "cunning." In the Hebrew, though, the literal meaning of that word is "prudent." I think this second translation is the better one. It suggests that the serpent was known not for his wiliness (for why, then, should Eve have believed him?) but rather for his caution and reliability. Eve would have placed the same kind of trust in that serpent as you might place in a judge. He had a good reputation around the Garden. He was not known for rashness.

Nor is there any indication that his speaking to Eve caused her surprise. On the contrary, they seem to have been familiar with each other, almost old friends. When

Eve listened to the serpent she was ready to hear wise counsel, common sense, reason. Perhaps, then, it was only by using the serpent that Satan could have broken down Eve's defenses. For she certainly knew the command of God. She knew the will of God. She knew the love of God. She knew the fellowship of God. Not without the greatest care and subtlety could Satan hope to persuade Eve to exchange divine knowledge for natural reasoning, to make her question the divine command. But he succeeded. And no sooner had he introduced the possibility of debate than he followed up by arguing, ever so gently, the case for the other side: Would Adam and Eve *really* die if they ate the fruit of the tree?

> *Then the serpent said to the woman, "You will not surely die. For God knows that in the day you eat of it your eyes will be opened, and you will be like God, knowing good and evil."* (Gen. 3:4–5)

Until this point it had never occurred to Eve that there was another way of seeing the issue. Now, though, she was exposed to another interpretation, an interpretation that not only differed from the first, but also (take note of this) appeared to have logic on its side. Why is this so important? Because in a debate, the most logical argument is the argument that *wins*. And what, at first sight, could be more logical than the idea that God had a hidden agenda in putting the tree out-of-bounds—that a bite of the fruit, far from inviting damnation, would lead to growth and enlighten-ment? Eve looked at the tree and saw that it was "good for food, that it was pleasant to the eyes, and a tree desirable to make one wise," so "she took of its fruit and ate" (Gen. 3:6). In truth, though, Eve was finished long before she looked. She was finished the moment she listened to the serpent's question, the moment she agreed to treat God's command as something to haggle over.

The same applies today. If the Enemy can get you to debate any of the issues that are settled in the Word of God, he's two-thirds of the way through. You're a dead duck. If he gets you to debate the rights and wrongs of cheating on your income tax, he's two-thirds of the way there. If he gets you to debate the rights and wrongs of emotional involvement outside your marriage, he's two-thirds of the way there. If he gets you to debate the rights and wrongs of compromising your faithful walk with God, he's two-thirds of the way there. Why? Because these issues have already been settled in the Word of God. There are plenty of things we can debate legitimately, plenty of areas where careful debate is not only allowable but necessary. But on the core issues of doctrine and morality God has already spoken, and there is no doubt about what he meant.

Let me give you five examples of issues that should be commands but have turned into debates.

(1) **Abortion.** The Enemy says, "Doesn't God really want every baby born into this world to be a wanted baby?" Accept that, and he's two-thirds of the way to making you a murderer. Why? Because *not* being wanted seems such a terrible fate that by comparison abortion looks like an act of mercy. Millions of babies are murdered each year in America because they are "not wanted." But since when was not wanting someone an excuse for killing him? God's command is clear: Thou shalt not kill.

(2) **Infidelity.** The Enemy says, "Doesn't God want everyone to be happy?" Accept that, and you're two-thirds of the way to getting a divorce. *Happiness* is a magic word in America. Everyone wants to be happy. Everyone feels it's a right. So what happens if you're not happy, if your marriage is making you miserable? Often the Enemy will put an easy solution in your way. He points to someone and whispers, "That woman over there, that man over there. If you want happiness, break free from your spouse and start again." Now I'm not denying that a marriage can end up in a heartbreaking mess, but if you put happiness before everything else you will not only persuade yourself into a divorce, you will probably wreck your next relationship too. That's how the Enemy works.

(3) **The Bible.** The Enemy says, "Surely a loving God would prevent suffering." Accept that, and you're two-thirds of the way to undermining the authority of Scripture. The

histories contained in the Bible are full of suffering and wars and inhuman cruelty. It is a fact that, in his wisdom, God does not immediately step in to prevent every murder of a child, every massacre, every act of injustice and exploitation. Nor is that what the Bible teaches. But many Christians do not want to find out what the Bible teaches. They'd rather put the Bible in golden covers, ceremonially parade it up and down the aisle at church, and daydream while Scripture is read to them. Nor, by and large, do the ministers help them(A large percentage of the mainline clergy do not believe that the Bible is God's self-revelation.)

(4) **Churchgoing.** The Enemy says, "Hell is just an invention of fundamentalist preachers." Accept that, and you're two-thirds of the way to being a backslider. After all, there are plenty of things to do with a Sunday morning besides going to church. You can entertain. Play golf. Read the papers. Go for a walk. In addition to which, the devil goes on, "How could a loving God seriously send anyone to hell? It's not as if you're actually *bad.* Just think of the billions of people who have rejected Jesus Christ. Do you think they're going to hell too? At least you're a member of a church. Your name is on the rolls. You go there once a year. If you end up in hell, you'll be in good company." And so today we have countless churchgoers, with their names on the church rolls, who deny the very heart and soul of the gospel.

(5) Women's ordination. The Enemy says, "God is a God of equality." Accept that, and you're two-thirds of the way to ignoring God's own principles of leadership. Nobody denies that men and women are equal in matters of salvation. In Christ, wrote Paul, there is no Jew and no Gentile, no male and no female (Gal. 3:28). But in the area of church authority the principle of equality collides head-on with Paul's teaching. The Bible is clear; there is no room for argument. Cling blindly to the equality principle, no matter what, and you will find yourself saying that Paul hated women, that he had a Jewish preoccupation with male leadership, and that we must distinguish in the Epistles between what Paul the apostle said and what Paul the Jewish rabbi said.

Fact #2: The Enemy Goes to Church

If you think the Enemy is going to come through the church doors and say, "Uh-uh, that's not a place for me," you are already deceived.

Satan has moved into many a church. He has introduced his own standards and gotten people to accept them. He has made his falsehood into their gospel. He has positioned his emissaries in their leadership. Someone said, "Satan is not fighting churches. He is joining them." It's true. For he does more harm by sowing tares than by pulling up wheat. He accomplishes more by infiltration than he does by frontal attack. After all, the most dangerous lie is the lie that resembles the truth. In this way the Enemy is able to use churches to pull people into his territory. These churches become fronts for his operation. They resemble real churches, live churches, but they are dead and they are staffed by false teachers. Let me tell you how they work.

There is a selling technique called the bait-and-switch method. To entice people into a store, the retailer advertises well-known brand-name merchandise for a very low price. But when the customer comes in to purchase that particular brand, he is regretfully informed it is out of stock. He is then offered an alternative—an inferior brand, which nevertheless costs more money. The brand-name item used to bring the customer into the store may never have been in stock at all.

Believe me, this is exactly how the Enemy works in churches. He sets up his phony leaders, his false teachers. They use biblical words, they use biblical terms, to capture and gain the seekers' ears. They talk about Christ, redemption, the Cross, the Resurrection—without believing in any of them. They do not submit to the gospel. They do not live under its authority. They use the language of truth because that is the language that draws people in. But there's no truth there, and there never was. When a seeker arrives in the church—just like the customer attracted by bait-and-switch advertising—he is confronted not with the true gospel, but with an inferior alternative, a pattern of belief and behavior contrary to the Word of God.

I have seen this in action. I once asked a West Coast minister, "Why do you so often use the phrase 'the risen Christ'?" In his liturgy and his sermons he always talked about "the risen Christ." I said, "Why do you keep using that term when you have told me that you do not believe that Jesus rose from the grave?" He said, "Very simple." (Actually it was more than simple, it was cold and calculated.) He said, "Number one, I believe that Jesus' soul is risen, just like every other dead person. But also, the few conservatives who give most of the money really like this stuff." He meant the believers. He called them conservatives.

Surprised? You shouldn't be. False teachers have been among God's people from the earliest times. What else were the Pharisees but false teachers? When Jesus came among them—Jesus the truth, the whole truth, the full embodiment of the truth of God—the Pharisees rejected him. Listen to what Jesus said to them: "You belong to your father, the devil, and you want to carry out your father's desire" (John 8:44b NIV). It is horrifying to think these words can be applied, no less aptly, to some church leaders today. They are false teachers, just as the Pharisees were. They preside over the same kinds of religious hierarchy. And they are taken in by the Enemy in just the same way.

The apostle Paul told Timothy: "Now the Spirit expressly says that in latter times some will depart from the faith, giving heed to deceiving spirits and doctrines of demons" (1 Tim. 4:1). As I spend time in fasting and prayer before the Lord, and as I look at the world and see what's going on, I am convinced in my own heart that Satan senses his end is near. He knows the time will soon come for his deception to be exposed and for him to be thrown into the lake of fire. And the closer we get to that time, the more he turns up the heat of deception. Christians are his primary targets. Satan is trying to take the strategic high ground in the church because from there he can divert people from the truth. It's happening even in the Sunday schools. Slowly, subtly, the truth of God's Word is being denied.

Watch out. And don't make the mistake of expecting too little of your leaders, for that is also a trick of the Enemy. I have a precious brother whom I love dearly. But he worships in one of those churches that denies the gospel of Christ. He called me one day, full of excitement, and said, "Listen, good news, good news!"

"What's happening?" I asked.

"Our minister," he said, "mentioned Jesus by name in the sermon yesterday. That is a positive step."

I must confess to you I did not know whether to be angry or to weep. Yet I find weeping to be much healthier than being angry, so I wept. Not only had the Enemy captured that church, he had so lowered the expectations of the congregation that even God's true believers expected nothing different.

Fact #3: The Enemy Wants to Meet Your Needs

How many times have I heard Christians in America say, "I wish I could find a church that meets my needs!"?

I want to tell you that this is deception, pure and simple. There is not a soul alive today who can meet your needs. The pastor can't meet your needs. The church board can't meet your needs. The Sunday school teachers can't meet your needs. Nobody can meet your needs except the Lord Jesus Christ. And yet people go along on a Sunday morning and ask themselves, *What can I get out of church? What benefit is there for me in this? Where is the payoff?* Their attention is focused entirely on themselves. But to have your needs met, you must first stop thinking about yourself. You must worship the living God, bow before him, honor and glorify him. You must say, "God, you are the Creator of the world, you are the Savior of my soul." Then, and only then, can your needs be met.

Nevertheless, many congregations have started to think of themselves as need-meeters. They have fallen into the Enemy's trap by asking what *they* can do as an organization to meet the needs of their members. Slowly they are starting to exclude God from the picture. They are like storekeepers who think they can satisfy the needs of their customers by showing them around the empty shelves. Ultimately the needs of those coming into a store are met by something that comes from elsewhere. The storekeeper does not sew the shirt, does not kill the cow and cut it into steaks. He simply sells the goods that somebody else puts on the shelf.

How many of us have had the experience of seeking something from a church but finding it like a store with nothing but empty shelves? For no church is perfect. You can always find fault. Maybe the children's ministry is not what you hoped it would be. Maybe the service isn't warm or lively enough for your tastes, or maybe it's too warm and too lively. Maybe the deacon hands you your hymn-book upside down. As long as you are expecting something from the other *people* at the church, you are going to be disappointed, and as soon as you are disappointed you will start to poison the fellowship with your dissatisfaction.

It is no coincidence that the New Testament makes so much of the tongue. James said,

> *But no man can tame the tongue. It is an unruly evil, full of deadly poison. With it we bless our God and Father, and with it we curse men, who have been made in the similitude [likeness] of God.* (James 3:8–9)

By gossiping and spreading rumors, by maligning others, by airing our grievances, by impugning others' motives and leveling false accusations, we give our tongues to the Enemy. We let him use them to destroy the fellowship of the saints. If a church is going to collapse or split, that is often how the process begins. So here again, remember the questions I put to you earlier: Who do you resemble?

Who do you imitate? The Enemy of your soul? Or the Lord of your life?

Fact #4: The Enemy Is a Supreme Forger

I used to think the Enemy's work would be clearly recognizable—that his methods would be unique and any territory he took would be clearly marked with his flag. I was wrong. I am not inexperienced; with the exception of one short eighteen-month period when I wandered off, I have been walking with the Lord since 1964, and have long had a gift of discernment. And yet, again and again, Satan's emissaries have sneaked up on me unawares—because the counterfeit product and the genuine article can look very much alike.

This is no accident. As we saw in the last chapter, the Enemy appears as an angel of light. His whole program is to emulate God. He wants people to think he *is* God. He even attempted to topple God from his throne. This failed, and God threw him out of the heavens as a result. But he continues to believe in his own divinity, and continues to insist that others believe in it too. And in a sense this is logical. For in that part of creation the Enemy controls, his powers resemble God's. That is why the Bible calls him "the god of this world."

The Bible gives us some clear examples of Satan's imitation. You can see it in the story of Moses before the pharaoh:

Then the LORD spoke to Moses and Aaron, saying, "When Pharaoh speaks to you, saying, 'Show a miracle for yourselves,' then you shall say to Aaron, 'Take your rod and cast it before Pharaoh, and let it become a serpent.'" So Moses and Aaron went in to Pharaoh, and they did so, just as the LORD commanded. And Aaron cast down his rod before Pharaoh and before his servants, and it became a serpent. But Pharaoh also called the wise men and the sorcerers; so the magicians of Egypt, they also did in like manner with their enchantments. For every man threw down his rod, and they became serpents. (Ex. 7:8–12b)

The next sentence reads, "But Aaron's rod swallowed up their rods." In other words, we are left in no doubt as to the shoddiness of the Enemy's workmanship. Nevertheless, we should not underestimate his ability to run a good advertising campaign. We are explicitly warned in the book of Revelation that the second beast, the Beast from the Land,

performs great signs, so that he even makes fire come down from heaven on the earth in the sight of men. And he deceives those who dwell on the earth by those signs which he was granted to do in the sight of the beast, telling those who dwell on the earth to make an image to the beast who was wounded by the sword and lived. (Rev. 13:13–14)

So if you are one of those Christians who runs around looking for miracles, be very careful. Miracles can be phony. People claiming to work miracles are a dime a dozen, and just because a miracle worker is standing in a pulpit does not guarantee that he is on God's side. Don't ever forget: The devil is a preacher. He is diabolical in his preaching, but he is a preacher nonetheless. He preaches another gospel, he preaches another Jesus, he preaches another power. And all of his demons have the same ability. They are all licensed and have credentials to preach. They will even concede a few peripheral doctrines in order to win your assent in denying the heart of the faith. They will cheerfully talk for hours on the importance of behaving in a godly manner, so long as they are not required to say that salvation comes only through the shed blood of Christ. That is the line they will never cross, because it is, in effect, the front line, the line dividing the forces of the Enemy from the forces of God.

In Acts, Elymas the sorcerer refused to cross that line. You will remember from Acts 13 that Barnabas and Paul had been preaching to Sergius Paulus, the proconsul of Paphos on the island of Cyprus.

But Elymas the sorcerer (for so his name is translated) withstood them, seeking to turn the proconsul away from the faith. Then Saul, who also is called Paul, filled with the Holy Spirit, looked intently at him and said, "O full of all deceit and all fraud, you son of the devil,

*you enemy of all righteousness, will you not cease per-
verting the straight ways of the Lord?"* (vv. 8–10)

The grounds of the conflict are clear. Luke, the writer of
Acts, has already said that the proconsul "called for Barnabas and Saul and sought to hear the word of God" (v.
7b). Elymas tried to turn this man "away from the faith."
He did not do it out of misplaced goodwill or by accident.
Paul saw straight to the heart of the issue when he
denounced Elymas as "full of all deceit and all fraud, you
son of the devil." That insight, we are told, came straight
from the Holy Spirit. It was Paul's gift of discernment. He
could see through the imitation. He could distinguish the
brand name from the cheap imitation, the copy from the
genuine article. It is a gift the Enemy prefers us not to
have, but one we need badly.

Fact #5: The Enemy Detests the Down-and-Out

Once I was walking downtown with a Christian brother.
We passed a wino sitting in a doorway. The knees of his pants
were worn through, and the soles were working loose from
his shoes. My companion heaved a sigh and remarked,
"Look at him. Don't you think that's Satan's masterpiece?"

I disagreed. The man was in a bad way, to be sure. He
was to be pitied, to be reached out to. But it is a gross mistake to think that the Enemy takes any special pride in a
piece of work like that. Far more likely, he reacts to a wino

with disgust and nausea. Why would someone who thinks he is God want to surround himself with derelicts from skid row? Satan may well think himself a great artist when it comes to molding human destinies, but to find his masterpieces you will have to look someplace other than the gutter.

Satan's masterpiece is someone who is upstanding, someone who is respectable, someone who is a community leader, *but who feels that he or she does not need Jesus Christ.*

Satan's masterpiece is someone who commands admiration, who is successful, who is strong and independent to the point of ignoring the claims of Christ.

Satan's masterpiece is the media personality who uses all the glamour of his or her position to tell us that true goodness means promoting gay rights and taking a pro-choice stance.

Satan's masterpiece is a bishop in the church who says, "The Bible is an archaic book. God will never judge anybody. Live any way you like."

You see, when Satan appears as an angel of light, it means he wants his followers to appear kind, gentle, and accommodating, to be into diversity, pluralism, and political correctness. More than anything else, to be *tolerant.* Note, however, that being tolerant generally *includes* all forms of sexual perversion but *excludes* godly living after the pattern of Scripture. Hence the outcry against prayer in public schools. Note also how the good work of Christian believers is ignored or taken for granted, while the media gives extensive coverage to the movie stars' charitable balls and concerts. Every day those who believe in the Lord Jesus Christ give themselves to others in selfless service. And yet this goes almost completely unacknowledged, while the crumbs that fall from the tables of the godless rich are greeted with fanfares, as though Hollywood alone could take credit for the world's salvation.

It is ironic that the philosophies espoused by followers of the Enemy—the philosophies of evolution and political correctness—are so woefully inadequate. They say, in effect, that men and women can make it on their own, that human perfection is attainable without the help of God. But what is happening as these philosophies tighten their grip on America? Turn on your television and you will see that the sociologists and other experts are baffled by the growth of violence, the rise in crime, the erosion of standards. All they can do is to recommend throwing more money at social problems. Raise budgets. Put more police on the streets. Pass more laws. Strengthen government. Set higher educational standards. None of which can do more than tinker with the problem, because their analysis of the problem is wrong. Their underlying assumptions are wrong. Humankind is not perfectible without the intervention of God. The answer to social problems is not to keep God out of public life; it is to let God back in.

But no. The Enemy now dominates the secular media. He wants to make his followers believe the lie that they can be perfect without having a relationship with Jesus Christ. In doing so he readily makes use of Christian values—

compassion, care, understanding—because these provide him with an ideal cover. After all, who would join his side if he was known to be planning the total ruin of those who serve him? He did not tell Eve that eating the fruit would get her thrown out of Eden. He only pointed to the fruit's advantages. It is in the Enemy's interests, therefore, to maintain the illusion that serving him is lucrative, that everyone has something to gain. Don't ever fall into the temptation of thinking that Satan is in the ghettos and the gutters. He assigns his most incompetent demons to those cases. His best work is to be found in the upper echelons, among beautiful people who are seeking to be perfect without Jesus. He is most often to be found with those who, like him, prefer to think themselves gods.

Fact #6: The Enemy Disguises Falsehood with Truth

Some time ago I read a story about a British art critic named Devine. Devine took his daughter to the ocean one day for a picnic, but he could not persuade the little girl to go with him into the chilly Atlantic waters. So he had an idea. He built a fire on the beach, and heated a teakettle with some water in it. When it had boiled he picked it up and with great ceremony poured the hot steamy water into the ocean. "Now it's warm, you can go in," he told his daughter. And the little girl ran gleefully in. What she saw was not an ocean full of cold water, but the kettleful of warm water. The story illustrates how the Enemy tempts us. He sprinkles the ocean of falsehood with a tiny drop of truth. But he does it with such a flourish, people see only the truth and not the falsehood—and so wade into it by the millions, not realizing they have been deceived.

Let me give you some examples of how the Enemy can use truth to deceive you.

(1) **In business.** Say you're a businessman or a businesswoman who is a Christian and wants to operate according to biblical principles. The Enemy comes in and says, "Good, good. Biblical principles are wonderful. They deserve our respect, and there is no doubt that in the past they have worked for all sorts of people." That's all true. But then he goes on, "Don't forget, though, that you live in the modern day. Things are different now. Everyone is a little closer to that bottom line. You have less room to maneuver. So if the competition cuts corners, you have to do the same. Blindly sticking up for principles will put you out of business. And God does not want you to be out of business, does he? He wants to bless you." It's the old argument that the end justifies the means. But it seems compelling. For what does a businessperson fear more than insolvency? And how many good causes—family, employee security, philanthropies—can a Christian businessperson point to that will suffer if the business slides?

(2) **In personal life.** Everybody has problems. If you are a Christian, you will take your problems to the Lord and seek his power and his wisdom to show you the way forward. But problems are seldom resolved with a snap of the fingers, and in the meantime you find yourself fighting uncertainty and discouragement and anxiety. Then the Enemy whispers in your ear: "Things getting tough? Need to forget your troubles for a while? Then have a drink." No sooner have you rejected this idea than the Enemy comes back at you. "Remember, drinking is biblical." Biblical? "Ever read Paul's first epistle to Timothy? 'No longer drink only water, but use a little wine for your stomach's sake and your frequent infirmities.' Read it yourself. It's right there in 1 Timothy 5:23. If the apostle Paul allowed drinking, surely it's okay." Here again, the Enemy is using truth. Paul *did* urge Timothy to drink a little wine. But there the truth ends, for a sip of wine taken for medicinal purposes is not the same thing as a couple of double scotches taken because life is getting on top of you. Don't be surprised if the Enemy quotes Scripture to you. After all, he quoted Scripture to Jesus during the temptation in the wilderness. And the Enemy knows his Scriptures well.

(3) **In dating.** Imagine a single person who has prayed fervently to God for a spouse, but whose prayers seem not to have been heard. The Enemy sympathizes. "God hasn't answered your prayer?" he says. "That's too bad." All true. And then he moves on from the truth to something else.

"Maybe you're not understanding God right. Maybe what he really wants you to do is to date an unbeliever. That way you get a date, and God gets a new convert. Anyway, dating is not the same as getting married. You don't have to talk about marriage. Just enjoy the dating." Let me tell you, I have met a lot of people who have taken this advice and bitterly regretted it. After all, we are not in control enough of our emotions to stop dating from turning into something more permanent. And being married to the wrong person is worse than not being married at all.

(4) In tithing. The Bible is absolutely clear about tithing. Tithing is like a tax. Would you dodge the IRS? Of course not. But countless Christians dodge God. They do not give anything like a tenth of their income to God's work. They listen to the Enemy, who whispers in their ears, "You know, God really doesn't need your money. After all, doesn't the Bible say he owns the cattle on a thousand hills?" Quite right. It does say that. But it also tells us to tithe. "Ah," the Enemy goes on, "but what about all those other God-given responsibilities you have? You must be prudent with your money. You need to have this particular house, you must have this particular car, you must have things for the kitchen and things for the dining room and things for the living room. Do you want to raise your kids without giving them all the material advantages their friends enjoy?"

That one hits hard, doesn't it? I was taking my second daughter to college some time ago, along with all the other parents. We were all unloading stuff: books, files, boxes, suitcases, clothes, pictures, stereos, CDs, computers. Every one of us seemed to have packed half a house in the back of the car. We lugged it all upstairs to our children's respective rooms—rooms so small that it was a struggle to get everything in. On about the second or third journey up the stairs, it struck me that we are a nation of things. We can't get along without things: things we really don't need, but can't bear to be without. And it's the parents as much as the children.

"After all," the Enemy continues, "you've got the future to think about. Pensions. Insurance. The mortgage. Holidays. God knows you can't cover all that *and* pay him 10 percent. Just put a couple of dollars on the plate when it comes around on Sunday morning, to show that you're doing your bit. Put a ten-dollar bill in if you want to look generous. But don't use the money you need for other things."

Of course this is a miser's philosophy. Give as little as you can to others, and save as much as you can for yourself. But what does the Bible tell us? It tells us we have turned the truth on its head. Certainly God does not need our gifts. He does not ask us to give for *his* sake at all. He asks us to give for *our* sakes. If we develop a giving, Christ-centered heart, if we learn to stretch the dollars we spend on ourselves so we have dollars left to give away, we will be blessed. It is that blessing the Enemy is so anxious to deprive you of—a blessing that will come not just financially but in ways you have not even dreamed of. Just read the prophet Malachi:

"Bring all the tithes into the storehouse,
That there may be food in My house,
And try Me now in this,"
Says the LORD of hosts,
"If I will not open for you the windows of heaven
And pour out for you such blessing
That there will not be room enough to receive it."
(Mal. 3:10)

Fact #7: The Enemy Never Attacks from the Front

There are some sins that every believer condemns. These are what might be called the big moral sins: unfaithfulness, unchastity, dishonesty, false belief. The big moral sins have an immediate impact because everyone agrees they are wrong and in most cases they are very clear-cut. Do you remember what happened in the 1980s when some Christian leaders were disgraced because of secret adulteries and underhanded financial dealings? Once those sins were out in the open, nobody could defend them. Nobody wanted to.

But there are other sins that never make the headlines. I call them the *socially acceptable sins*. They are socially acceptable because most of them are so widespread, Christians have covered them with a conspiracy of silence. And yet the socially acceptable sins have the greatest long-range negative impact upon you, your family, and the body of Christ.

They are sins that express conflict in our ordinary day-to-day relationships at home and at church. Sins that happen between husband and wife, children and parents, colleague and colleague, church member and church member. Sins like:

- Gossiping and murmuring
- A critical spirit
- An unforgiving heart
- Rebellion against God's principles in marriage and home
- A husband's abdication of spiritual responsibility in the home
- A wife's resentment of her husband's spiritual leadership
- A child's refusal to obey parents
- A desire for self-promotion
- Putting others down
- Spiritual pride and jealousy
- Divisiveness and rebellion against spiritual authority

For example, you may think you are having a prayer meeting. But listen to what is being said in and around the prayer. Are you really praying together, or are you getting together to gossip and complain? You may think you are having a counseling session. But listen to what is being discussed. Is it any more than an airing of resentments and bitterness? And what about that sermon? Were you hearing

God's truth proclaimed from the pulpit, or was this really an exercise in self-promotion and spiritual pride? Because of these socially acceptable sins, situations in which believers ought to be coming closer together in the Spirit instead become points of friction and disharmony.

Listen carefully to the words of Jesus. In the hours before his trial and crucifixion, on his knees in the Garden of Gethsemane, he prayed one of the most significant prayers recorded in the New Testament. He prayed to his Father for all his disciples, those already living and those yet to be born,

> *that they all may be one, as You, Father, are in Me, and I in You; that they also may be one in Us, that the world may believe that You sent Me.* (John 17:21)

The phrase *that they all may be one* occurs twice in this one sentence. Jesus was asking that believers be *one* together, and that believers be *one* with God. For only in that oneness will the world see as well as hear the gospel. The unity of believers is the greatest demonstration of the love of God. That unity, that oneness, is what will bring sinners to Christ. Not just preaching, though the Word must be preached if it is to be believed, but living out the Word in the unity of the church.

Now if you are ever tempted to think Satan is stupid, think again. Satan is not stupid. He knows exactly how to counter the evangelization of the world. He knows because he has studied the Bible very carefully—more carefully than many Christians have. He knows that one of his main objectives in stifling the gospel must be to undermine the unity of Christians. So he does everything in his power to accomplish that. Whenever husband and wife have an argument and go to bed without forgiving each other (or at least resolving to deal with the issue), Satan has succeeded. Whenever two believers in Jesus Christ are in ongoing conflict with each other, Satan has succeeded.

Yet if the Enemy relied only on frontal assault, if he came in his true colors, discerning believers would get together on their knees before God and start praying. And God will give them victory. But the enemy is too crafty to use a frontal assault.

Let me tell you a helpful story I heard during my boyhood in Egypt.

It is said that in the fifth century a famous holy man used to spend much time at prayer in the desert, just as Jesus did. Like Jesus, this holy man suffered temptations. So righteous was he that the devil sent a whole posse of demons on a special assignment to trip and entice him—in short, to do whatever it took to make this man of God fall. They used all the usual methods. Lustful thoughts to drag down his spirit. Fatigue to keep him from prayer. Hunger to make him abandon his fasts. But no matter what they tried, or how hard they worked, again and again their efforts came to nothing. In the end Satan was so annoyed at the incompetence of his minions, he pulled them off the project and took over himself.

"The reason you have failed," he lectured them, "is that you used methods too crude for such a man. He will not fall to a direct assault. You must be subtle, and take him by surprise. Now watch the master at work!"

The devil then approached the holy man of God, and very softly whispered these words into his ear: "Your brother has been made the Bishop of Alexandria."

Instantly the holy man's jaw stiffened. His eyes narrowed. His nostrils flared. Bishop of Alexandria! His brother! What an outrage!

Now this is a legend, not history. But it makes an important point. Notice that the demons who tempted the holy man got nowhere by using the big moral sins. He could see them coming a mile off, and could defend himself. So what did Satan do? He used a socially acceptable sin. He even tailored it to the man's particular weakness. He knew that this man was guarding against the temptation of the flesh, and that it was futile to try to ambush him that way. So he sneaked up using envy and spiritual pride. He made him think, *Hey, I'm the godly one in the family. Why is my brother getting to be the Bishop of Alexandria, and not me?*

So watch out for the socially acceptable sins. Satan knows that if he comes out in the open and fights a biblically sound, Christ-loving church, he will lose. So he will not even try. Instead he will attack from another direction.

He will infiltrate the churches with people who have spiritual pride, people who are possessed with critical spirits, people who are seeking self-promotion, people who cannot distinguish between a true angel of light and the fallen angel masquerading as an angel of light. And through them he will begin to sow the seed of doubt. He will begin to sow the seed of discontent. He will begin to sow the seed of division and partisan spirit. And before you know it, the church's leadership will be running around trying to put fires out, and losing their fire for God and the gospel.

One of the Enemy's most potent tactics is to *divide and rule.* It is one that worldly powers have used successfully down the ages, as in 1980 in the Iran-Iraq War. Many in the U.S. government were anxious to take sides. But more mature advice prevailed. "Let them exhaust each other," many counseled, "so that neither side will have energy left to turn on the West." It was a later policy of supporting Iraq against revolutionary Iran that laid the groundwork for Iraq's invasion of Kuwait.

Believe me, the Enemy does not make mistakes like that. His pattern in the Christian church is to divide and rule, divide and rule. There were times at the General Council of my father's denomination in Egypt that I wondered whether this was a general synod or a Mafia meeting, so vehemently did the delegates shout and denounce one another. I thought perhaps it had something to do with Middle Eastern culture. But when I moved to Australia, where I lived and ministered for eight years, I found Christians

KNOW YOUR REAL ENEMY

there fighting just as hard—only more politely. What Satan wants us to do is to stop fighting as soldiers of the cross, and begin fighting as soldiers of our own opinions. For then the war turns inward, and we begin to destroy one another instead of fighting our real Enemy.

K N O W

THE

Y O U R

ENEMY'S

R E A L

CHAIN

E N E M Y

OF COMMAND

JOHN VAUGHN of the International Mega-Church Research Center and Southwest Baptist University in Bolivar, Missouri, was on a flight recently from Detroit to Boston.

He had not paid much attention to the man in the next seat, but noticed after a while that the man had bowed his head and was moving his lips as if praying. When he finished Vaughn said, "Are you a Christian?"

The man seemed shocked. "Oh, no," he said. "You have me all wrong. I am not a Christian. I am a satanist."

Curious, Vaughn asked what he had been praying for.

The man said, "Do you really want to know?"

Vaughn assured him that he did, and the man told him. "My primary attention is directed toward the fall of Christian pastors and their families living in New England." He paused. "And what's your business in Boston?" he asked Vaughn.

"I'm editor of the *North American Society for the Journal of Church Growth*. I'm going to Boston to do a pastors' seminar."

Vaughn outlined his ministry and its purposes for the kingdom of God, and shortly afterward the satanist indicated that he needed to return to his work!

Does that story alarm you? It should. Peter Wagner, in whose book *Prayer Shield* this encounter is recorded, documents how all over the North American continent satanists are gathering for the specific purpose of praying against evangelical Christian leaders. They concentrate on key pastors across the land and target them for failure. They have networks of prayer to Satan, each one taking responsibility for a particular region. They pray for the families of leading evangelicals to break up.

Why *leading* evangelicals? The answer has to be that the Enemy knows the importance of a command structure. We are not just using descriptive language when we talk about the church as an army and Christians as soldiers of Christ. The church is indeed a fighting organization. It follows a battle plan and needs strong, insightful leaders to coordinate its campaigns. Satan knows full well that when a pastor falls, the ripples spread far and wide through the

Christian community. If a solitary man sins, he alone suffers the consequences. Much better, then, from the Enemy's point of view, to go for a person of influence—the family man, the community leader, the national politician. For the corruption of such an individual melts down through his whole field of influence. The wider that field of influence is, the greater the damage caused by the sin. Who can forget Adolf Hitler, who not only ruined Germany but flooded almost the whole continent of Europe with the misery of Nazi repression?

The Enemy understands command structures because he himself operates one. The demonic hierarchy, in fact, closely shadows its angelic counterpart. Satan, too, is fighting a war. He, too, has his generals and his field commanders. He, too, maintains order and discipline to assist his twin aims of harassing Christians and keeping the unsaved spiritually blind. His forces are rebels who have broken away from God's angelic army, taking with them not only their weapons but also their ranks and divisions.

Satan is a copycat. He has copied the angelic order. In organizing his demon hordes he has not created anything new, for he is incapable of creating. He has only stolen ideas from elsewhere. In this way, Satan and political liberals have a lot in common. The liberals in this country never establish great institutions. They never start great schools. They only hijack them from the godly men and women who founded them. That is the Enemy's way. But ironically, it has one advantage for us. If we want to understand the

Enemy's organization, we can find no better way to start than examining the genuine article: the hierarchy of angels from which Satan broke away.

THE HEAVENLY HOST

We use the term *angel* frivolously. We say to someone, "Oh, you are an angel." We tend to say it most often to women, little girls, and babies. And we usually say it when they have done something that pleases us. I have yet to hear a parent call a child an angel when he is screaming his head off or throwing food at the dinner table. At such times parents use other words, but not *angel.*

From this you might suppose that angels are female, fragile, relatively weak, and concerned mainly with doing minor good works. This certainly is the way they are portrayed in many books and films. Somehow we have gotten into the habit of imagining angels with halos and wings—an image supplied not by the Bible, but by old religious paintings and Christmas cards. Most believers do not understand the nature of angels. They do not understand the activities of angels. They do not understand the form of their existence. They do not understand the purpose of the angelic realm. Most, in fact, know so little about real angels that meeting one would give them a heart attack. Why else would the angel announcing Jesus' birth to the shepherds have begun by saying, "Do not be afraid" (Luke 2:10)? The truth is, angels are not effeminate harpists dressed in bed linen: They are God's marines.

Here are five things you need to know about angels.

(1) Angels have individual personalities. Since the *Star Wars* films we have become familiar with the New Age idea that good exists in the universe as a nebulous supernatural force. But this is far from the truth. The heavenly host is not impersonal, nor is it a single entity. Each angel is an individual person, with an individual job to do. Remember how the Christmas story begins:

> *Now in the sixth month the angel Gabriel was sent by God to a city of Galilee named Nazareth.* (Luke 1:26)

Not *an angel,* but *the angel Gabriel.* This angel had a name and a mission. Explaining the actions of God seems to be Gabriel's specialty, in fact, since we know he was also sent to talk to Daniel. Daniel said,

> *And I heard a man's voice between the banks of the Ulai, who called, and said, "Gabriel, make this man understand the vision."* (Dan. 8:16)

From the Word of God we know that angels possess personality, intellect, feeling, and free will. They have different functions, but their primary responsibility is to administer the will of God, to execute the plan of God in our lives as we submit to the lordship of Jesus Christ.

(2) Angels never die. Every angel God ever created is alive today. Gabriel's appearances to Daniel and Mary, separated by hundreds of years, indicate that angels are not bound by human time spans. Also, Jesus told us that angels live according to different physical laws. Answering the Sadducees' question about divorce, he said,

For in the resurrection they neither marry nor are given in marriage, but are like angels of God in heaven.
(Matt. 22:30)

He did not mean that men and women *become* angels—that lame idea comes from watching too many sentimental television dramas. But we become *like* angels in that we enter a realm where death does not exist. Because the angelic ranks are not depleted by death, there is no need for a system of marriage and reproduction to keep their number constant.

(3) Angels have bodies. Wherever they turn up in the Bible, angels have a physical form. "Suddenly there stood before me," said Daniel of Gabriel, "one having the appearance of a man" (Daniel 8:15b). That word *appearance* is important. The celestial body is not like ours. It is a different kind of body, designed for a different kind of realm, working according to different rules. But, like our own, it has form and likeness and weight. Yet it is capable of much more.

We see Jesus clothed in such a body after his resurrection. Though Jesus reassured his disciples that he was not a disembodied spirit—"Handle Me and see, for a spirit does not have flesh and bones as you see I have" (Luke 24:39b)—it is clear he did not need to unlock the door to get into the room. In Luke's words, "as they said these things, Jesus Himself stood in the midst of them" (Luke 24:36a).

Celestial bodies can also travel great distances at high speed. Daniel records that

> *while I was speaking in prayer, the man Gabriel, whom I had seen in the vision at the beginning, being caused to fly swiftly, reached me about the time of the evening offering.* (Dan. 9:21)

We see the same with the resurrected Jesus. One moment he was in Galilee, the next moment in Jerusalem. One moment he was talking to Mary outside the tomb, the next he was going to see his Father before returning to the Upper Room. The facts here are stranger and more wonderful than any fantasy put out by Hollywood. And while we're on the subject, don't fall for all that *Ghostbusters* nonsense about blasting evil spirits with bolts of electricity. <u>The celestial body is indestructible</u>.

Angels even *look* different from people. Sometimes the difference is minimal, which is why Daniel described his visiting angel as the "man Gabriel." Usually, though, an angel will be an awesome sight. Daniel described another angel in this way:

> *His body was like beryl, his face like the appearance of lightning, his eyes like torches of fire, his arms and feet like burnished bronze in color, and the sound of his words like the voice of a multitude.* (Dan. 10:6)

So terrifying was this angel that his presence affected even those who had not seen him. "A great terror fell upon them," said Daniel, and "they fled to hide themselves" (Daniel 10:7b). In one of his novels, C. S. Lewis pictures a visiting angel as a shaft of brilliant light so straight that it makes everything else in the room look curved. Be cautious of anyone who speaks lightly of meeting angels. If you meet an angel, you will *never* forget it.

(4) **Angels have different ranks.** When God began his work of creation, he did not start with the earth. He started with the angelic realm. Genesis says, "In the beginning God created the heavens and the earth" (1:1). Writing to the Colossians about Christ's role in creation, Paul the apostle used the same ordering: heavens first, earth second—

> *For by Him all things were created that are in heaven and that are on earth, visible and invisible, whether thrones or*

dominions or principalities or powers. All things were cre-
ated through Him and for Him. (Col. 1:16)

Incidentally, a lot of those people who say, "What I cannot see does not exist," are going to have egg on their faces when God finally unveils the invisible world and everyone can see it. But notice the four terms Paul used here to define the angelic hierarchy: *thrones, dominions, principalities,* and *powers.* Remember those four words, because I will come back to them again and again. Paul placed the ranks in descending order of seniority: *thrones, dominions, principalities,* and *powers.* The powers occupy the lowest level. They are the foot soldiers, the ones sent to execute the purposes of God. Above them the angelic hierarchy sits like a pyramid, each level exercising a wider sphere of influence than the one below it. At the top is God, who executes his will and supervises the administration of his universe through the ranks of his angels. That is why the Old Testament so often refers to God as the Lord of hosts. He is the Commander in Chief of countless angelic battalions. At his word, the whole army moves. At his command, vast numbers of angelic beings obey.

Clearly God is a God of order. God is a God of rank. God does not work on the principle of equality, with the leader being only first among equals. He uses a chain of command. He loves order, and when things get *out of order* you can be sure Satan is responsible. In its structure the angelic hierarchy is similar to a corporation. If you work in a big company you may want to bear that in mind. The next time you are tempted to complain about your boss, or your boss's boss, or your boss's boss's boss—just remember that God has placed you there. Just as important, remember that God has placed *them* there. Your task is to serve the living God. The company may pay your salary, but you offer your labor as unto the Lord.

(5) Angels have specific jobs. In another way, however, the angelic hierarchy is very *unlike* a corporation. In many corporations, particularly at the lower levels, people tend to lose their individuality because they are all doing much the same thing. They become instruments in the production process. But not only are no two angels the same, no two angels' *jobs* are the same. Each angel God sends out has a distinctive role in the mission to protect, preserve, and take care of his elect.

One of the most crucial jobs angels do is to frustrate the Enemy's campaign to depopulate heaven. If it were all up to Satan, he would prevent every man and woman on earth from coming to the saving knowledge of the Lord Jesus Christ. And whenever someone slips through the net—whenever someone accepts Christ as Savior and begins to live the Spirit-led life—Satan tries his hardest to ensure this person remains ignorant both about himself and about the Word of God. Ignorance is a powerful weapon in Satan's armory. God's angels, then, often do the work of bodyguards, fighting off attacks and keeping channels of communication open. Every day unseen spiritual battles are being fought over your head.

For He shall give His angels charge over you,
To keep you in all your ways.
In their hands they shall bear you up,
Lest you dash your foot against a stone. (Ps. 91:11–12)

Isn't that exciting? I was born a nobody, and yet God had a plan for me. He assigned his angels to look after me. They countered my foolishness when I thought I could reach God my own way. They countered my ignorance. They steered me around the traps the Enemy had laid to prevent my coming to know the Lord Jesus Christ as Master of my life. And after that, the angels continued to watch over me day and night. I don't know about you, but that thought thrills me—especially when I get behind the wheel of my car. I don't often preach on bad driving—it's too convicting—but a few weeks ago I took two of my colleagues in the car with me to make a pastoral visit. They later told me they had actually seen my angels at work!

God uses angels to perform miracles in your life. Do you know that there are hundreds of miracles happening around you every single day, and you're not even aware of them? God has commissioned his angels, and said, "Go down. Take care of her. This is my daughter. Take care of him. This is my son." Look carefully at the Bible and you will find angels popping up in all kinds of places, fulfilling a mission to protect God's children. Shortly after the Holy Spirit came on the church, the apostles were imprisoned by the Sadducees.

> *But at night an angel of the Lord opened the prison doors and brought them out, and said, "Go, stand in the temple and speak to the people all the words of this life."* (Acts 5:19–20)

Later on, Peter was imprisoned by Herod, and kept under guard, chained between two soldiers.

> *Now behold, an angel of the Lord stood by him, and a light shone in the prison; and he struck Peter on the side and raised him up, saying, "Arise quickly!" And his chains fell off his hands. Then the angel said to him, "Gird yourself and tie on your sandals"; and so he did. And he said to him, "Put on your garment and follow me."* (Acts 12:7–8)

Later, when the angel had completed his assignment by escorting Peter to the nearest intersection, he disappeared.

> *And when Peter had come to himself, he said, "Now I know for certain that the Lord has sent His angel, and has delivered me from the hand of Herod."* (Acts 12:11a)

So much for angels. What about Satan and his army?

THE INFERNAL HIERARCHY

We saw earlier that when Lucifer's pride got the better of him and he rebelled against God, he was thrown out. The attempted coup failed. Or did it? That's not the only way of looking at it. Satan may not have toppled God, but on the face of it he significantly altered the balance of power in heaven. The day after the battle, no less than a third of God's angels went AWOL and transferred their allegiance. John referred to this event in picture language when he wrote:

And another sign appeared in heaven: behold, a great, fiery red dragon having seven heads and ten horns, and seven diadems on his heads. His tail drew a third of the stars of heaven and threw them to the earth. (Rev. 12:3–4a)

John imagined Satan as a dragon, lunging with his tail as he fell from heaven and dislodging a third of the stars from the sky. The stars refer to the angels. In reality the fall of Satan was not a solitary protest. It was a big-time rebellion. And no doubt it is on the basis of his unprecedented "success" in this first battle that the Enemy projects his ultimate victory. A third of the heavenly host are already behind him. The rest, he assures himself, must soon follow.

How did Satan persuade so many of the angelic beings to join him? Earthly revolts give us an insight into the kind of horse trading that was going on in the corridors of heaven. Lucifer would have offered all kinds of incentives. He would have promised the equivalent of promotions and bonuses, stock options, a company jet, free skiing in St. Moritz, and a key to the executive washroom. Every rank—thrones, dominions, principalities, and powers—would have been offered an appropriate reward. Nothing has changed in that respect. Countless millions of people throughout the world today still fall for those same lies. The same Enemy promises the best and pays the worst. He promises honor and pays with dishonor. He promises pleasure and pays with pain. He promises profit and pays with loss. He promises life and pays in the currency of death. It's the same Enemy. And a third of all the heavenly host went with him. But just in case this begins to look like a formidable achievement, let us keep things in proportion. Even if one-third of the heavenly host joined the opposition, it still means that for every demon harassing you there are two angels to give you protection. Glory to God!

What else do we need to know about the Enemy's infernal hierarchy? Three things.

(1) The Enemy's forces retain all their God-given powers. You see, when Lucifer was thrown out of heaven, he set up his kingdom and government on the only model he knew. He had been right there in the presence of God. Day and night he had been before the throne. He had observed how God worked. So that's what he copied. He patterned his own administration after God's. In Ephesians 6:12, the famous passage about spiritual warfare, Paul wrote the following:

For we do not wrestle against flesh and blood, but against principalities, against powers, against the rulers of the darkness of this age, against spiritual hosts of wickedness in the heavenly places.

Notice that the fourfold hierarchy of angels described in Colossians is mirrored almost exactly in this fourfold hierarchy of demonic forces: *principalities, powers, rulers of the darkness,* and *spiritual hosts of wickedness.* This is no accident. The titles vary a little, but the structure is exactly the same. Four levels of demonic leadership, with Satan at the top (or, if you prefer, at the *bottom*). <u>Satan may have lost his innocence when he fell, but he did not lose his intelligence</u>. Like their heavenly counterparts, these fallen angels all have their own personalities. They have their own distinct characteristics. They are immortal and are not limited by time or space. The difference is that they worship Lucifer instead of the living God.

(2) The Enemy has agents on your case. Keep in mind that although Satan stands at the head of a hierarchy, and although he thinks himself divine, he is not God. His minions may have the same capabilities as the heavenly angels, but Satan cannot fully emulate his Creator. For example, he is not omnipresent. Unlike God, who is present throughout his creation, Satan cannot be everywhere at the same time. He cannot be at your house and at my house at one and the same moment. So what does he do? Simple. He uses his demons. With the exception of Christ's temptation, where he turned up in person, Satan does not perform day-to-day temptation and harassment any more than the CEO of Microsoft or General Electric would answer calls at the company switchboard. He leaves such routine matters to his underlings.

But do not relax your guard on that account. These creatures will do anything they can, try any ploy at their disposal, to harass you, to frustrate you, to oppress you. Paul said that our fight is not against flesh and blood. That's true. But neither is it against a vague principle of evil, as the liberals would have us believe. Demons are conscious, active, and deeply committed to their task.

We are not dealing with people who punch the clock at 8:00 in the morning and then punch out at 4:30 in the afternoon, after a half-hour lunch and two coffee breaks. We are not dealing with people who take six months' vacation twice a year. We are not dealing with people on welfare, able to sit back and wait for their next government check. I wish we were. However, demons are well disciplined, well armed, and blindly obedient soldiers of Satan. You have to be vigilant. You cannot afford to say to yourself, "Now I can let my guard down for a moment, because Satan and his demons are somewhere else." Demons have a lot of advantages. Possessing spiritual bodies, they are not limited to space and time. They can dog your footsteps, lay traps for you, shadow you everywhere you go. They will try to undermine your plans. They will invade your prayer life. They will interrupt your thoughts. They will hinder your testimony and discourage you in every way they know how. And very often they will use your friends and family to do it.

(3) The Enemy is within. A man went to a costume party some years ago dressed up as the devil. He had on a full-length red leotard, complete with horns and a tail. On his way to the party, his car broke down on a country road. The only light he could see came from a building across the field, a church, so he set off to knock on the door, forgetting how he was dressed and thinking, *These Christian folks can help me fix my car.* As soon as he stepped through the door though, everyone panicked. They rushed through the windows and out the back door, until only one person was left—a little old lady, standing there defiantly with her cane. He looked at her. She looked at him. Then she pointed her cane at him and said, "Now listen, devil. I may have been a member of this church for fifty years, but I've been on your side all that time!"

Now, I don't think many old ladies in our churches are conscious emissaries of the devil. But many Christians of all ages and backgrounds allow themselves to be used by the Enemy.

It is the saddest thing. Christians who do not resist the devil, who do not flee from temptation, are in effect fraternizing with the Enemy. Have you thought about that? In any regular army, assisting the enemy is an act of treason. You get court-martialed and shot. Yet how many Christians are guilty of spiritual treason? How many Christians act in a way that wounds or troubles other believers? Perhaps it's not deliberate; they would probably be shocked to know that a demon helped put the thought into their minds. But that's the way it is in the invisible war. We are not only soldiers, we are also the battleground.

After I preached this message at The Church of The Apostles one time, a close friend and founding member of the church came to me afterward and said, "Do you think Satan was using me ten years ago when I told you not to start this church?" It was not my place to answer the question directly. But I quoted to him the passage from the Gospels where Peter, in all good faith, tried to prevent Jesus' death on the cross:

> *Then Peter took Him aside and began to rebuke Him, saying, "Far be it from You, Lord; this shall not happen to You!" But He turned and said to Peter, "Get behind Me, Satan! You are an offense to Me, for you are not mindful of the things of God, but the things of men."*
> (Matt. 16:22–23)

Peter had not planned to go against his Master. And although he was "mindful of . . . the things of men" in this attempt to prevent Jesus from dying, he certainly had not figured the Enemy into the equation. Nevertheless, Satan was using him. And if he can use Peter, surely he can use any of us.

LIVING IN THE WAR ZONE

By now you may be thinking, *This is frightening.* And it is—to someone who does not belong to Jesus. But it should not be frightening to the child of God. This is the most important news. Because the faithful servant of God—who is not quenching or grieving the Holy Spirit, who is not living in constant disobedience to God and to the Word of God—has God's angels watching over him and empowering him to go from victory to victory. You may not be able to see them, but God's angelic beings are surrounding you. They are executing the will of God on your behalf. They are faithfully standing beside you to preserve you, to keep you, to sustain you until you get to heaven. Why? Because you are an heir of salvation, you are a prince or princess, a child of the King.

Does the Enemy's organization hold any lessons for us? I think so. Our knowledge of the Enemy's command structure should immediately encourage us in two areas.

(1) Prayer. In my office I have a painting, given to me a few years ago by my daughter Sarah. It shows a father kneeling beside his son's bed, praying. Outside the window demons are trying to get in, but an angel of the Lord is blocking their way. As a parent I want to convince you of the importance of prayer. Get on your knees. Pray for your children. Intercede for them and offer the sacrifice of praise and thanksgiving for them, even as Job did, because when you do that the angels of God will foil the demons' plans. As long as you are faithful in prayer, the Enemy can do them no harm.

Have you ever read that in a book on parenting? Not in any book I've seen. I have nothing against books. I love books. I write books. And I would advise parents to read as many as they can get their hands on. But there is a whole set of spiritual issues that most parenting books simply do not address. So when I hear someone say, "Oh, Dr. So-and-so has come up with a new book that tells you everything you need to know," I get suspicious. Read all the books you can, but recognize that if you do not spend time on your knees, praying, interceding, and even crying before God, you cannot give your children the help and protection they really need.

(2) Obedience. We do not have balance in the Christian community. On one side we have people in the mainline church, and beyond the mainline church, who prefer to think Satan and his hordes do not exist. On the other side we have a group of people who say, "All you need to do is cast out demons, and everything is fine." Clearly the second view is closer to the truth. But stating it that way gives the impression that once the demons are cast out, everything will be hunky-dory and the devil will not so much as sneeze in your direction until you reach glory. Take my word for it: Satan is not so easily scared off. Before you know it he will be up and at you again, and he will get the better of you if you have not made a thoroughgoing commitment to Jesus Christ and closed all those doors I talked about earlier.

I decided to write this book to put forward a balanced and biblical view of the Enemy, a view that affirms the existence of the devil, but also affirms that obedience will close him out. In other words: *expect* that Satan will attack you, but don't lock the front door to your soul while leaving all the windows open. Because if you have a weak point, Satan will find it. For example, no matter who you are or how long you spend in prayer, sooner or later a demon called *past sins* is going to come knocking. He will do this by stirring up memories of all the things you have done wrong in the past, either reminding you of how enjoyable they were, or making you feel guilty about them. Here is how you deal with him. Remind *him* of something. Remind him of his future, because the Bible says that the lake of fire was specially prepared for the devil and his angels. *Your* past sins don't matter. *His do.*

KNOW YOUR REAL ENEMY

Similarly, if a demon comes along whose name is *fear*, take up the sword of the Spirit and tell him about the promises of God for you (Ps. 118:6; Luke 12:32; Heb. 13:5–6).

When a demon called *worry* comes to you and loads you with the cares of this world, tell the Enemy, "My Jesus said not to worry about tomorrow, because tomorrow will worry about itself" (see Matt. 6:34). That's how you have the victory.

The thing you *should not* do is forget about Satan, any more than a soldier at the front can afford to forget about his counterpart on the other side of the line. If you blithely go your way, working hard, not spending time with the Word, playing hard and hardly praying, you will find that in a very short time—weeks, even days—demons have come through the doors you have left open. Before you know it, your Christian life will be collapsing like a soufflé.

Obey. Do not take the mercy and grace of God for granted. Do not give room to the Enemy to work in you and through you. But if you do, remember that all is not lost. For that is another illusion the Enemy would like to sell you. No Christian is perfect. We all progress in the kingdom by a winding path. What matters is to line up behind your Commander in Chief. If you step out and get hit, do not stay there. Do not have a pity party. Just get back in line and say, "Forgive me. I'm going to walk behind you again"—and God will give you the victory.

Every time he catches you out, the Enemy unintentionally does you a favor: He alerts you to a weakness in your defenses. So when you stumble, take it to God. Ask, "Lord, what's going on. He will show you something in your life that is not lining up with his will, something that allows the Enemy a place to enter. Then close the doors. No one in the Enemy's chain of command can break down a closed door.

PART TWO

KNOW HOW THE ENEMY FIGHTS

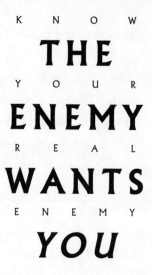

KNOW

THE

YOUR

ENEMY

REAL

WANTS

ENEMY

YOU

AT THE end of his first epistle, Peter, the earliest leader of the church, wrote these words:

Be sober, be vigilant; because your adversary the devil walks about like a roaring lion, seeking whom he may devour. (1 Peter 5:8)

Those who know the world of wild animals say there are three occasions when a lion roars. First, he roars when a competitor strays onto his territory and tries to hunt there. The roar says to intruders, "This is my territory. Get out of here. Stay out."

Second, he roars if he's caught in a storm. Apparently lions dislike the crash of thunder and the flash of lightning.

Third—and this is what I believe Peter was referring to in his epistle—the lion roars after he has caught his prey. He has brought an animal to the ground, and he roars his triumph. He is saying, "I've got you!"

You could conclude from Peter's words that we Christians are perched in a tall tree with the devil roaring at us from below, just as dogs bark at a cat they cannot reach. But this is not the way lions behave. Lions do not roar as they are stalking or chasing their prey. They never announce their arrival by trying to frighten the prey. Their method is to get as close as they can without being seen— so close that even if the quarry sees them it's too late—and then to pounce. The devil "walks about," the New King James Version tells us. Other versions of the Bible put it more accurately. "He prowls," they say. Quietly. Cunningly. Waiting for his moment. Saving his roar until he has his victim pinned down and there is no escape.

The image of Satan that Peter gave us is not a comfortable one. It isn't meant to be comfortable. It's meant to keep us on our toes.

SATAN THE ADVERSARY

If your faith in God and Jesus Christ is genuine, Satan is your enemy, whether you like it or not. You cannot just keep your head down and pretend the conflict is not happening. You are in the middle of it! Satan is *your* adversary. You and I developed this adversarial relationship with Satan the day we said yes to Jesus. At that very instant of surrender, you antagonized Satan. You insulted him. By being snatched from the jaws of death and hell, you have kicked Satan in the teeth—and he will never forgive you for it.

There is no neutrality in Satan's attitude toward you. He thought he had you in the bag—but now you're free. When someone escapes from his realm, Satan does not just shrug his shoulders and say, "Never mind, he won't be missed." On the contrary, he will go after you with a vengeance. Literally. Not in person, of course, for remember that Satan is not omnipresent and cannot be everywhere at once. But he *does* have countless demonic assistants, and he is well organized. So he will enlist demons to work on your case and will devise strategies to win you back.

You probably sense this already. If your experiences are anything like mine, you'll agree with me that the Enemy greets you every single morning, and keeps working on you every hour of the day. He uses his fallen angels to dog you and create havoc in your life. He wants to stop you from living a life of faith, to stop you from living a life of obedience to God and his Word. He wants to separate you from the provision of God, the mercy of God, and the grace of God.

KNOW YOUR REAL ENEMY

Always remember that you are in enemy territory. I said in the last chapter that the Bible calls Satan *the god of this world.* That's exactly right: in this part of the created order, Satan rules. Christian believers are an invading force. We have established a beachhead, established a foothold, but danger is all around us. Never forget that we are surrounded by unseen adversaries, and they are seeking to destroy us.

You get in the car with your spouse, and the devil is there. When your spouse is sitting beside you, the Enemy is in the middle—even if you can't see him. You go to church, and he's right there with you. Some people think they leave the demons outside when they go to church. Forget it. Satan and his hordes go in there with you so they can start talking to your mind. As the Word of God gets planted in your heart, Satan tries to snatch it away. It may be happening to you right now, as you read this book. These demons are saying to you, "Don't believe this stuff about Satan. He doesn't really exist. You've got enough problems without having to worry about a personal devil. Just forget about it. You're a decent person. You don't have to worry about Satan."

Beware of negotiating with Satan. You run the same risk a hunter did one day when he saw a huge grizzly bear. He lifted his gun to his shoulder and was about to pull the trigger, when the bear spoke. To his surprise, it had a soft, almost hypnotic voice. The bear said, "Hey, isn't it better to talk than to shoot? Why don't we sit down? Let's negotiate this matter. What do you really want?"

The hunter lowered his gun. He thought about it, then said, "Well, all I really want is a fur coat."

"A fur coat?" replied the bear. "No problem. That's good. I think it's something we can talk about." He went on, "For my part, all I want is a full stomach. Really, I'm hopeful we can reach a mutually satisfying compromise."

And so they talked it over. They started negotiating.

You don't parley with Satan any more than you sit down to discuss terms with a grizzly. The idea that everyone has a bit of the truth and all we need to do is fit it together like a jigsaw puzzle has brought the mainline church to its knees. Because <u>Satan is not really interested in compromise</u>. It's just his way of ensnaring us. Which is why, after a little while, the talk between the hunter and the grizzly came to an end, and the grizzly was seen leaving on his own. Through negotiation he had managed both to fill his stomach and give the hunter a fur coat. How? Simple.

The grizzly had eaten him.

<u>Satan means business</u>. When you and I go to sleep at night, he's still burning the midnight oil, making plans for the next day. In the middle of the night the lion is still prowling, pacing up and down, hungry, determined to get his prey. After all, lions don't stalk their quarry for the fun of it. They don't sneak up on us so we can take

photographs of them. The devil is waiting for you to grow spiritually lazy—and when you do, he will move with lightning speed. Right after he brings his prey under him, he will roar, as if to say, "I've got you!" He will roar the roar of victory, which will tell everybody else, "Stay out of here! She's mine! He's mine! Now leave me alone so I can enjoy the fruits of my kill!"

That roar is a challenge to Almighty God. Satan says, "God, look at the devastation I've brought on one of your children." For remember, Satan's aim, from his first rebellion, has been to take God's place. "I will exalt my throne above the stars of God," he said. "I will be like the Most High." He has never given up that ambition. And every battle, every skirmish he wins in the invisible war, every success he scores in undermining your faith and witness, makes him more certain that one day he will achieve his ultimate goal. In his delusion, he thinks he has taken another step closer to removing God from the throne so Satan can rule the universe himself.

This is why Peter gave us this essential advice: "Be sober, be vigilant; because your adversary the devil walks about like a roaring lion."

Why did Peter say to be sober? We're all aware of the misery caused by drunk driving. I have buried young people who were its victims, and it is heartbreaking beyond words. Drunk driving is the number one killer on our roads. A drunk person is incapable of accurately assessing his ability to drive safely. He has impaired vision. He has impaired reactions. He has impaired control of his limbs. And yet he *feels* like a superman. Drunkenness creates the ultimate form of self-deception. Sin, said Peter, is *like drunkenness.* It can numb our spiritual senses to the point of making us deny the existence of a spiritual war. People who are not spiritually sober are unable to see things clearly, from God's perspective. They do not live by a set of biblical values.

Peter told believers to be serious-minded about the devil. To be serious-minded about the invisible war. To be serious-minded about the traps the Enemy sets up to ensnare the unwary. Do not be flippant about the Enemy if you are a child of God and walking with Jesus Christ. Do not be flippant, because the Enemy wants to destroy you, to destroy your family, to destroy your business, to destroy everything you touch. That's his intention. He wants *you.*

But of course you are not the *only* one the Enemy wants. Christians and Christian leaders down through the ages have been the focus of his attention, and plenty of prominent believers in Scripture have fallen to Satan's temptations.

PROMINENT BELIEVERS HAVE ALSO FALLEN

Let's look at some of the believers in the Bible who gave in to Satan.

Joshua Lost Because He Was Overconfident

Everyone knows the story of Joshua and the battle of Jericho. How the people of Israel came up to take this strongly fortified city. How God gave Joshua the instruction not to attack head-on, but to march around Jericho seven times—a strange military tactic, to say the least. And how at the end of seven circuits the Israelites blew their trumpets, and the city's fortifications collapsed.

Yet not so many have read what happened next. The Bible tells us:

> So the LORD was with Joshua, and his fame spread throughout all the country. But the children of Israel committed a trespass regarding the accursed things. (Josh. 6:27—7:1a)

Flushed with victory, unaware of the sin in Israel, and feeling overconfident, Joshua sent spies up to the next city. Just how blasé the Israelites had become can be judged from the spies' advice, and Joshua's credulity in following it. The spies said,

> Do not let all the people go up, but let about two or three thousand men go up and attack Ai. Do not weary all the people there, for the people of Ai are few. (Josh. 7:3b)

Joshua underestimated both the resilience of the men of Ai and the devastating impact of Israel's sin. The raiding party was repulsed with thirty-six fatalities, and Joshua was reduced to despair. He fell before God and cried out, "O Lord, what shall I say when Israel turns its back before its enemies?" (v. 8). God, though, brought this self-pity quickly to heel. "So the LORD said to Joshua: 'Get up! Why do you lie thus on your face?'" (v. 10).

The source of the problem was soon uncovered. During the plundering of Jericho, one of the Israelites had gone against God's specific command and had committed a sin of greed. He finally confessed:

When I saw among the spoils a beautiful Babylonian garment, two hundred shekels of silver, and a wedge of gold weighing fifty shekels, I coveted them and took them. (v. 21a)

The Israelites quickly found these items, which cleansed the people of their sin. Ai fell soon afterward.

You might think that was the end of the episode. But no sooner had Joshua routed Ai than he was fooled into signing a treaty with the Gibeonites. Once again Joshua acted impulsively. The people of Israel did what they thought was best, but "they did not ask counsel of the LORD" (Josh. 9:14b). The results of this mistake were severe. Joshua should have destroyed the Gibeonites, but by swearing in the name of God that he would spare them he tied God's hands and compromised Israel's long-term security. You can almost hear the roar of Satan: "I got your man. I got your man."

Success and overconfidence go in the motion of a pendulum. One swings into the other, and back again. Beware when you have scored a victory over the Enemy; that is precisely the time when you are most at risk.

Joshua fell into temptation. So did that great man of God, King David.

David Fell Because He Ceased to Be Vigilant

I advise you to spend a few minutes reading 2 Samuel, chapter 11, because it will teach you a lot about temptation. If ever a man seemed to deserve trust, loyalty, and confidence, it was David, a man blessed by God, a man distinguished for being "after God's own heart," a king of Israel at the peak of his powers. And yet in this passage we see him behaving in a way that was not only unstatesmanlike but downright villainous. He made a single satanically inspired decision, and from that determination flowed a foul river of lust, covetousness, adultery, intrigue, betrayal, and, finally, murder.

His decision is described in just five words: "But David remained at Jerusalem" (2 Sam. 11:1b). Doesn't sound like much, does it? David took some time off. He let Joab, his chief of staff, take care of destroying Ammon and besieging Rabbah while he went back to his palace. The Bible does not give us a reason. Maybe David was tired. Maybe he had other business. Maybe he wanted to test Joab's leadership qualities. We just don't know. But however innocent the motives, this decision was fatal. It took David away from his primary responsibilities of leadership, and he ceased to be sober and vigilant. He did not hear the lion creeping toward him. He was not prepared for the temptation. But one night he couldn't sleep. He got up—and the trap was there, ready to spring.

I want to ask you a question. When you have a sleepless night, what do you do? Do you get up and watch television, or do you get on your knees and begin to bless God and pray? Do you allow your mental VCR to rehearse the past day's problems, or do you sing praises and bless the name of God?

Almost every day we are presented with options like this. Every moment that is not consciously dedicated to some godly end is available for the devil to use. It is like blank space to doodle in, a silent interlude to be filled with noise. That's why one of the best ways to avoid being tempted is to fill your mind and attention with some positive and constructive project. If David had walked across the street, he would have been in God's temple. He would have been safe. But no:

> *David arose from his bed and walked on the roof of the king's house. And from the roof he saw a woman bathing, and the woman was very beautiful to behold.* (2 Sam. 11:2b)

The whole sorry tale of David's sin unfolded from that moment. He made inquiries about the woman (v. 3a).

He discovered her identity (v. 3b). He slept with her (v. 4). She got pregnant (v. 5). He attempted to disguise his adultery by bringing her husband, Uriah, back from the war and getting him drunk so he would sleep with her (vv. 6–13). Finally, when Uriah proved more pious than David and refused to sleep with his own wife lest he endanger the war effort, David cold-bloodedly arranged his death (vv. 14–25).

By then, however, David had long been in Satan's control. When he walked up the stairs to the roof of the king's house—when his eyes fell on the woman and his heartbeat quickened—Satan sprang his trap and roared, "God, I got your choicest." After that, the rest was inevitable. I will not dwell on the consequences. Suffice it to say that, through a moment's loss of sobriety and vigilance, David brought tragedy to his kingdom and dishonor to the name of his God.

Joshua fell, David fell, and so did Simon Peter.

Peter Fell Because He Underestimated His Character Flaws

If you are ever tempted to think you've blown it—that Satan has finally and irrevocably dragged you away from God—reflect on the life of Simon Peter.

Peter's faith was strong and straightforward. And at the end of Jesus' earthly ministry, after Jesus had gathered his disciples around him for the Last Supper, Peter

expressed that faith with typical enthusiasm and thought-
lessness. "Lord," he said, "I am ready to go with You, both
to prison and to death" (Luke 22:33). They had just
shared the precious Passover meal, in which Jesus had
revealed that he himself was the Passover Lamb, and that
he was going to die for the redemption and salvation of
humankind. But this was not what inspired Peter's out-
burst. Right before he affirmed his faith in Jesus, the
Lord had said:

Simon, Simon! Indeed, Satan has asked for you, that he
may sift you as wheat. But I have prayed for you, that
your faith should not fail; and when you have returned
to Me, strengthen your brethren. (Luke 22:31–32)

If you're a city slicker, you may not appreciate what is
meant by that phrase *sift you as wheat.* That is not an
enjoyable process. The sieve is a round implement made
of wood, about twenty-four inches in diameter, sometimes bigger, with a fine wire mesh across the bottom.
The person doing the sifting puts the wheat into the
sieve, along with the chaff and the dirt and everything
else, and then begins to shake it vigorously, throwing the
contents into the air so that the chaff can be blown away.
In Peter's case—so Satan's request implies—very little
wheat would be left. And even with Jesus praying for him,
the sifting was pretty thorough.

KNOW YOUR REAL ENEMY

I do not have to tell you what happened. During Jesus' trial, Peter, who had promised to go with Jesus to prison and to death, was so scared that he denied even *knowing* his Lord and Master. And he did it—not once, not twice, but three times—as Jesus had predicted. "Immediately, while he was still speaking, the rooster crowed" (Luke 22:60b). Peter had fallen right into Satan's trap, despite Jesus' warning. He had been vigilant for his Lord, but not vigilant for his own weakness of character. You can almost hear the lion's roar behind the cock's crow. Satan was shouting, "God, I've got the chief apostle of your Son. I've got him!"

Peter, the Bible tells us, went out and wept bitterly. Yet his sifting had just started. After the sifting of fear came the sifting of self-doubt and self-hatred. I wonder if Peter thought of suicide. He had betrayed his friend in a way that was not much different from Judas. He had become utterly useless.

Isn't that exactly what it's like to be depressed? As if life has come to an end. How many Christians have been trapped in those feelings? But note that Peter knew how to repent, unlike Judas, who by now had scattered his thirty pieces of silver and hung himself. Repentance is the answer. "When you have returned to Me," Jesus said, "strengthen your brethren." Peter clung to those words, and after the Resurrection, he obeyed them.

Let's look at one more example—one of the most disturbing instances of satanic attack in the New Testament.

Ananias and Sapphira Fell Because They Purposely Disobeyed

We read in the book of Acts, chapter 5, that the believers were selling their possessions and putting the money at the feet of the apostles. They were giving everything, for these were trying times. Their enemies were throwing Christians out of their houses, out of their jobs, and out of their communities because of their faith. They had no option but to rely on one another for everything. Most of them had witnessed Jesus' resurrection. And you would think that if any group of people deserved to be called sober and vigilant, this would be it. Yet two of them, a man by the name of Ananias and his wife, Sapphira, sold a piece of land and then secretly withheld a portion of the proceeds. They had accepted Jesus as their Lord and Savior. They were committed enough to sell their land, but they were afraid. They wanted security. They left open the doors of fear and lying, and the Enemy got in.

Listen to what happened when Ananias tried to lay his gift at the apostles' feet:

But Peter said, "Ananias, why has Satan filled your heart to lie to the Holy Spirit and keep back part of the price of the land for yourself? While it remained, was it not your own? And after it was sold, was it not in your own control? Why have you conceived this thing in your heart? You have not lied to men but to God." (Acts 5:3–4)

Unlike David, whose initial sin seems to have been unpremeditated, Ananias and Sapphira sinned deliberately, with careful preparation. Also their sin appears to have had more immediate and more dire consequences, for "Ananias, hearing these words, fell down and breathed his last" (v. 5a). The same fate befell his wife three hours later. This raises an important question: Can Satan really devour God's children, even depriving them of their salvation?

The story of Ananias and Sapphira is ambiguous on this point. But turn to the first epistle of John. "We know that whoever is born of God does not sin," wrote John, "but he who has been born of God keeps himself, and the wicked one does not touch him" (1 John 5:18). A fuller translation of the word *touch* is "sever the vital union." In other words, John said Satan cannot break the cord of salvation linking the Christian believer to God. Even the careless believer, the believer who repeatedly forgets to be sober and vigilant, cannot lose his salvation. God has spoken, and Satan is powerless to change it. *But*—and this is a big but—Satan can devour almost everything else. Your peace of mind. Your effectiveness. Your witness. Your health. Your friendships. Your marriage. Your work. Everything. All of this can be devoured by the roaring lion. The devil not only roars, he has teeth. He can chew you up so thoroughly, your entire Christian life is a write-off.

Peter did not write, "The devil is a paper tiger." Paul did not say to the Ephesians, "Lay aside the armor of God, you won't need it." James did not tell Christians, "Don't bother resisting the devil, he'll never even come near you." Instead we are urged over and over again to resist the devil, to be spiritually sober and vigilant, to put on the armor of God, to live every day in God's fullness, and to pray every day in the Spirit. On the basis of those commands, we have authority over the devil.

I have often heard a statement attributed to the great German Reformer Martin Luther that advises us to make fun of Satan: "The best way to drive out the devil, of course, is through using the Scripture, but if he will not yield to the text of the Scripture, then jeer at him, flout him, for he cannot bear scorn." After all, it is Satan who is going to end up in the lake of fire, not us. Ultimately the joke is on him.

Yet the enemy has not given up; he works very hard to keep us weak.

HOW THE ENEMY KEEPS US WEAK

Many Christians in America are stuck in neutral and are unproductive. They are saved, but their Christian walk is going nowhere, like a car with its wheels mired in the mud. This is profoundly satisfying to the Enemy. Countless troops in God's army have never received their basic training. They're standing on the drill square, flabby, undisciplined, lazy, and afraid.

From the Enemy's point of view, Christians like this are his highest achievement. We learned earlier that Satan cannot undo the work of salvation in a believer. God has spoken, and Satan is powerless to countermand the order. So the Enemy aims for the next best thing—not the believer's soul, but the believer's *effectiveness*.

If you could peek at Satan's goal-setting program, you would find that one of his prime objectives is to keep Christians from growing in faith. To keep them from understanding and applying the Word of God in daily life. To keep them in the murky, shallow waters of mediocrity, to keep them focusing on their problems, on their pain, on their worries, on their own little kingdoms. Why? Because these Christians will never pose a threat to him. They are soldiers who can't shoot, fighters who can't fight.

Jesus warned his followers of this in one of the best-known passages in the Gospels. If you think you know this parable so well that you don't need to read it again, I advise you to pick up your Bible and find Matthew 13:1–9, 18–23. You might be surprised at my interpretation of the parable of the soils.

The Parable of the Soils

I can hear you correcting me. Most translations and commentaries entitle this passage The Parable of the Sower. But it is not about the sower. Nor is it about the seed. Very emphatically the focus of Jesus' message is on the *soil*.

There is a good reason for this. Both the sower and the seed are beyond the Enemy's power. The sower is God himself. The seed is God's Word. And the writer of Hebrews told us that

> *the word of God is living and powerful, and sharper than any two-edged sword, piercing even to the division of soul and spirit, and of joints and marrow, and is a discerner of the thoughts and intents of the heart.* (Heb. 4:12)

It may surprise you to know that Satan agrees with this. In that sense he is a believer—not because he submits his will to the Holy Spirit (that he absolutely refuses to do), but because bitter experience has proved to him what the Word of God can do. He knows it can change our lives. He knows it can convict us of sin. He knows it can judge and condemn us. He knows it can encourage and uplift us. He knows it can accomplish God's purposes in our lives. Satan does not mess with God's Word any more than you or I would mess with a stick of dynamite.

So the Enemy uses a different tactic. He can't change the sower. He can't change the seed. So he monkeys around with the soil where the seed has to take root, constantly seeking to prevent the Word of God from taking root and growing in Christian hearts.

Three kinds of soil serve the Enemy's purposes:

Soil #1: Seed-Proof Soil

Archaeologists excavating one of Egypt's famous pyramids once discovered a grain of wheat. When they ran tests, they discovered to their surprise that this grain of wheat had been inside that pyramid for nearly three thousand years. All this time it sat there on a hard rock, doing nothing. Yet someone has calculated that if that grain had been planted and harvested, planted and harvested over the same period of time, it would have produced enough bread by now to feed the entire planet for two days!

Look carefully at the first part of the parable, as explained by Jesus:

> *When anyone hears the word of the kingdom, and does not understand it, then the wicked one comes and snatches away what was sown in his heart. This is he who received seed by the wayside.* (Matt. 13:19)

The phrase *by the wayside* is significant. This soil is not in the middle of the field—it is on the edge. In other words, this is liable to happen to people who keep themselves on the fringes of the church.

What is the nature of such soil? Well, I don't know much about American farming, but I can tell you a little about farming in the Middle East, which Jesus had in mind when he told the parable. Over there, fences or hedgerows do not separate one farm from the next. Between Mr. Hussein's farm and Mr. Ali's farm you will find a narrow pathway, a strip of land, which the repeated pressure of feet and hooves has compacted into such a hard crust that even rainwater fails to penetrate it. In its natural state this kind of soil is not ready to receive seed. If any seeds fall on it, they just sit there, exposed, unnourished, unshaded, waiting like peas on a dinner plate until a hungry bird swoops down and eats them.

Notice how Jesus explains this part of the parable. This kind of soil is like the people who *hear* the Word of God, but *do not understand it.* They get some goose bumps around Christmas time. They get teary-eyed when a tragedy strikes somewhere. Otherwise their hearts are as hard as rock. They may go to church on occasion. They may even read the Bible. But nothing is getting through.

Perhaps these "waysiders" figure they know everything the Bible says already, so they don't need to listen. Perhaps they have such fixed ideas about God, they refuse to listen to anything new. Perhaps they can't concentrate for more than a few seconds. Or, it may be they forget what they've heard as soon as they hear it. All these subterfuges are part of the Enemy's strategy to produce hardness of heart. And none of us are immune. With the help of his demons, Satan will try to make sure that God's Word flies in one ear and out the other. He will try to stop us from applying the Word of God to an upcoming business decision. He will try to make us substitute human wisdom for God's Word, psychology for scriptural teaching, or counseling for the power of the Holy Spirit. In all these ways he will attempt to snatch the seed of God's Word from us before it has the chance to grow and bear fruit.

He will do this very quickly. If you have visited the Middle East, you have noticed the ravens. They go around and around, searching for something to take, then suddenly—*whack!*—they snatch it and fly off. Those who have the spiritual seed snatched from them in this way may develop a sense of restlessness and dissatisfaction. I have known people who go from church to church, from teacher to teacher, from counselor to counselor, from seminar to seminar, from retreat to retreat—yet nothing is happening inside. Satan has convinced them, "All you need is more seed, more seed, more seed," when in reality the problem is not the seed but the soil. They need the plowing of the Holy Spirit to break up the soil of their hearts and allow the Word of God to take root.

How does this first type of soil turn seed-proof?

(1) Through sin. The psalmist said, "If I regard iniquity in my heart, / The Lord will not hear" (Ps. 66:18). If there is a sin in our lives, and we've rationalized it, all the teaching and preaching in the world will not do us any good. The only way forward is confession and renewal. That's why we start our worship with confession, so we can break the hard soil of our hearts. If there is any hardening there, confession begins to break it down so that God's Word will be able to penetrate.

(2) Through bitterness. The writer of Hebrews warned Christians against the "root of bitterness" (12:15). It's an apt description, for bitterness goes down deep into the soil of our hearts. Some plants in the desert areas of the Middle East have adapted to their dry environment by sending roots down though the rocks—forty or fifty feet deep!—to tap subterranean moisture. Such roots are not easily dislodged. Similarly, to harbor bitterness toward another person creates a fundamental change in the depth of your personality. You become so wrapped up in the injustice you claim has been done to you, you can see little else. Even the Holy Spirit will have trouble getting through. The Word of God will glance off you even if you read it twenty-four hours a day.

(3) Through compromised leadership. The average church in America has around 250 members. If the devil wants to reach out to a whole church, he is going to need a minimum of 250 demons to do it—one demon to snatch the word from each believer's heart. But the devil is a great economist. It's so much more economical to go after the preacher. He will make him preach a lie, while at the same time convincing people that they are hearing an honest exposition of God's Word. That way Satan uses just one demon to achieve exactly the same result. He gets 250 people for the price of one.

That is one reason ministers of the gospel find themselves under particular attack. A friend told me recently of a struggle at his church. The minister had been in the same pulpit for twenty-five years. He wasn't preaching a lie, but familiarity with the congregation had left him complacent, and he was no longer challenging or inspiring the membership with the Word of God. Still many members gave him their unqualified support, and when those who could see what was happening felt it was God's will for him to move on, the argument between the two sides almost split the church. Satan was right there, dividing and conquering.

Where Satan's first plan fails, he has a second plan in place: the principle of shallow soil.

Soil #2: Shallow Soil

If Satan cannot prevent the seed from germinating, he will do his best to prevent the soil from nourishing it, leaving the seed vulnerable to extremes of weather.

But he who received the seed on stony places, this is he who hears the word and immediately receives it with joy; yet he has no root in himself, but endures only for a while. (Matt. 13:20–21a)

This is the person who gets excited about the gospel. He comes down the aisle, signs the decision card, and goes to church for several months afterward. Every time the doors are open, he's there. And then his weakness is exposed:

For when tribulation or persecution arises because of the word, immediately he stumbles. (Matt. 13:21b)

Receiving the Word carries a cost. Family members begin to make fun of you. They'll say, "Hello, Mr. Preacher" or "Here comes the prophet." Or a colleague at work will find out you have committed your life to the Lord, and he will start telling everyone, "Hey, watch out, here comes the Bible-thumper. Be careful." These remarks are particularly damaging to young people, who are so vulnerable to peer pressure. Their friends tell them, "Well, you're not cool anymore. You're no fun to be with."

Nobody enjoys persecution. So why endure it, if it can be avoided? That is what a demon will whisper in your ear. "You know, the smart move is to go underground with your newfound faith. Don't flaunt it. Keep it quiet. That way you won't upset anyone." I've even heard ministers say: "You need to keep your religion between you and God. After all, religion is meant to be private." Tempting, isn't it? Especially if a church leader gives his stamp of approval. But keeping your faith secret erases your effectiveness for God.

I've seen it happen. Some years ago a couple said to me, "We're leaving your church."

I asked why.

They said, "Our children are not saved, and when they come home and bring their friends at the holidays, we just find it very embarrassing to take them to The Church of The Apostles. The preaching is so blunt and so hard. We want to take them to a church where they'll hear some abstract sermons."

Now as a father of four children I can tell you right out that I would rather see my kids offended and in heaven than appeased and in hell because of abstract sermons. An unsaved person needs to be told he's as lost as a goat in a hailstorm, and that he needs Jesus Christ. If he finds that offensive, God bless him. I can't help that. My obligation is to preach the gospel.

Seed-proof soil, shallow soil—if those don't work, Satan uses a third method to keep believers weak: spoiled soil.

Soil #3: Spoiled Soil

As the sower scattered his seed, the parable tells us, "some fell among thorns, and the thorns sprang up and choked them" (Matt. 13:7).

The soil here is perfectly good. It isn't hardened or shallow. It is soft, deep, well-watered. By rights, the seed should thrive in it. And this is exactly why the Enemy works so hard to prevent the seed from growing. His strategy? Make sure there are plenty of *other* seeds in the soil, ready to compete with the seed of the Word. As Jesus explained:

He who received seed among the thorns is he who hears the word, and the cares of this world and the deceitfulness of riches choke the word, and he becomes unfruitful.
(Matt. 13:22)

We usually think of the thorns as worries and material ambition, ensnaring people who cannot let go of their anxieties or who seek security in their net worth rather than in their commitment to Jesus Christ. Most often, though, the thorns are simply *activities*. Look around the average church, and you will find Christians who are busy, busy, busy—with nothing to show for it. You see, if Satan cannot snatch the seed of the Word away from your heart, if he cannot stunt its growth with persecution, then he will get you so wrapped up in activities, you won't have time to think about growing or reproducing yourself in the kingdom of God. Satan will open up a new job possibility. He will expand your social life. He will get you to play the stock market. He will give you prominence and fame, or co-opt you onto another committee. None of these things are bad—not even the committee. But they are all distractions from our first goal: to grow and bear fruit.

I speak from experience. In the first two years of The Church of The Apostles, I was run ragged. Finally, in the fall of 1989, the Lord put me flat on my back for two weeks. I couldn't carry on with my activities. Confined to my bed, I had no choice. And the Lord's precious voice was so clear to me. He said, "You cannot minister to others until you have ministered to me."

That blew me away. I thought I was doing my best. I thought it was my *job* to minister to others. I don't mean I missed my devotions. Even at the busiest times I read the Scripture every day. I prayed. But you see, I had a problem saying *no*. I took on everything that came my way. And the Lord had to tell me that no matter how hard I worked, I wasn't the fourth member of the Trinity. He also had to remind me that the Holy Spirit did the *real* work; I'd better get my priorities straight because one hour spent in harness with the Holy Spirit achieved more than a year slogging it out on my own.

I can tell you for a fact that ministers are the biggest culprits when it comes to going it alone. The average evangelical American pastor spends less than twenty minutes a day in prayer. His counterpart in Korea spends at least ninety minutes. Is it any wonder that God is doing great things in Korea? The Lord took me away from my activities and made it clear to me that he wanted me to give the first two hours of the day to him—and him alone. If I had not obeyed, if I had not adjusted my lifestyle radically, I honestly believe I would not be around to write this book today.

Activism is Satan's trick, pure and simple. He delights in getting us preoccupied. It doesn't matter what the object of that preoccupation is. Good things will serve just as well as evil. All the Enemy wants is for our attention to be distracted and our strength sapped. And in most of America his strategy is working. Having lived in three different cultures around the world, I am convinced that Americans think that activity and productiveness are the same thing. It's not that activity is wrong, any more than riches are wrong. Activity is fine as long as it does not become the focus of your life. Riches are fine as long as they do not become your security and your primary goal. God has given us many good things to enjoy. It is our responsibility as Christians to make sure that we use them correctly, and do not treat them with a single-minded devotion, which turns them from gifts into idols.

Let me tell you something about idols. When the Muslim general Mohammed Ghusani invaded India, his forces went into the Hindu temples and smashed every idol they could find. Islam does not tolerate idols—and, of course, Hinduism has many of them. Entering one celebrated temple, Ghusani was confronted by the priests. They pleaded with him, "We beg of you, do not destroy the idol here. This is the holiest of all idols. Please leave it alone." Ghusani took no notice. Pushing the priests aside, he unsheathed his sword, and dealt the idol a resounding blow. Immediately it shattered—and a stream of precious stones cascaded from its hollow center.

Our idols are not made of wood or plaster, but they are just as real, and we cling to them just as tenaciously as those Hindu priests. Yet every time we destroy an idol, we gain far more than we lose. For every idol we demolish will bring us new treasures of grace and remove another hindrance to the productive life of prayer.

An effective Christian walk, in which idols are readily disposed of, comes from a soil in which the seed falls, roots, germinates, and bears fruit.

But he who received seed on the good ground is he who hears the word and understands it, who indeed bears fruit and produces: some a hundredfold, some sixty, some thirty. (Matt. 13:23)

This good soil belongs to those who are sober and vigilant, those who are serious-minded about the Enemy and the Enemy's works. They are productive according to the talents and blessings God has given them. They are not all productive to the same degree or in the same way, but their productiveness is in line with God's wider plan for his kingdom. The Enemy wants to neutralize this productiveness, so that the forces ranged against him will be weaker. It is part of our calling as Christians, therefore, to strive to be good soil.

So it's necessary to do some soil testing in your life. If you come to the Word of God with an unrepentant heart, Satan is going to snatch the seed away. If you come to the Word of God harboring bitterness or a fear of being unpopular, your faith will wither. If you come to the Word of God preoccupied with anxieties and activities, your productiveness will be choked. But as you develop a strong and nourishing soil, the good seed of the gospel sown by the Lord Jesus Christ will produce genuine and abundant fruit. When that happens, the Enemy's plan is foiled.

As Christians we *have* to walk in daily submission to Jesus Christ. In that and that alone resides our authority over the devil. We can't be cocky. We can't single-handedly take on the spiritual principalities and powers. The devil, the roaring lion on the prowl, can be defeated only by the power of the Lord Jesus Christ and the blood of the Lamb. For only when you and I line up behind that other, greater lion, the Lion of Judah, and are covered by the shadow of the Almighty and fortified by the whole armor of God, can we expect to be victorious.

CHAPTER 5

KNOW

CLOSE

YOUR

COMBAT

REAL

WITH THE

ENEMY

ENEMY

DURING THE Second World War, immediately after the collapse of France, Hitler pushed westward to the coast of the English Channel and prepared his assault on the British mainland. He knew that if he was to send ground troops across to invade Britain, he would first have to win the war in the air. And so the Battle of Britain began. Nazi Germany sent massive formations of bombers over British territory, attempting both to destroy ground installations and to knock out the British air defenses. If Germany won air supremacy, the invasion would be easy.

Against these massive forces, the British fighter command used a number of strategies. One of the most important was this: keep above the enemy. Gain higher altitude. Fight from above. So when the radar warned of an imminent attack, and the order came for crews to scramble, Royal Air Force pilots took their planes up as high as they could, as fast as they could. It was one of the reasons Britain won the air battle, and why the invasion, when it came, was an Allied invasion going the other way—from Britain into occupied France.

Fight from above might summarize God's instructions to his people in the invisible war. Because *above* is where Christ is. Turn to Ephesians and see how Paul prayed that Christians might understand

> *what is the exceeding greatness of His power toward us who believe, according to the working of His mighty power which He worked in Christ when He raised Him from the dead and seated Him at His right hand in the heavenly places, far above all principality and power and might and dominion, and every name that is named, not only in this age but also in that which is to come.* (1:19–21)

When God raised Jesus from the dead, he gave him, in spiritual terms, the highest altitude possible. He sat him above "all principality and power and might and domin-ion"—in other words, above the entire angelic order, good and evil. He sat him above Satan and his demonic forces. He sat him high above circumstances and chance. He said to Jesus, as the psalmist recorded, "Sit at My right hand, / Till I make Your enemies Your footstool" (Ps. 110:1b).

Now you may think this puts Jesus rather far off. After all, there is no higher place than to sit at God's right hand. If ever Scripture gave us an image of the transcendent God, this is it. But look at what Paul went on to say in the next chapter of Ephesians:

> *But God, who is rich in mercy, because of His great love with which He loved us, even when we were dead in trespasses, made us alive together with Christ (by grace you have been saved), and raised us up together, and made us sit together in the heavenly places in Christ Jesus.* (2:4–6)

Take a look around you. Where are you? Sitting in an armchair? Out on your veranda? In an airport or a bus station someplace? Forget it—in the reality of the Spirit you are in none of these places. You are up there with Christ Jesus. Those who belong to God, who are born of the Spirit of God and have surrendered their lives to Jesus Christ, are already positioned in heaven. Physically you may be on earth, but spiritually you are with God. Isn't that wonderful? That is the blessing God has given us. Unlike the RAF pilots of the Second World War, we have altitude already. We don't have to jump into airplanes to achieve it. We're already there. As heirs of the everlasting kingdom we already occupy ground that is inaccessible to the Enemy.

We are already in that one place from which we can successfully attack and resist the devil. From this vantage point we make Satan and all his minions vulnerable. We have the victory because we are where Christ is.

THE ENEMY'S TACTICS

How does the Enemy hope to attack and overcome you when you are, in effect, beyond the range of his biggest guns? Let me give you another example from the pages of military history.

Not many people have successfully invaded the British Isles. Hitler failed. Napoleon failed. In fact, to find the last time anyone brought an army across to British shores you have to go back to the year every school student in Britain knows by heart—the year 1066. At that time what we today call England was populated by the Anglo-Saxons and ruled by King Harold. You probably know the story already. The Normans crossed the channel under the leadership of William the Conqueror, trounced the Anglo-Saxons at the Battle of Hastings, during which Harold took an arrow in the eye, and then proceeded to overrun the country.

What many people don't know is that the Battle of Hastings was a very close contest. Harold was no pushover. He had carefully positioned his troops at the top of a long ridge, giving them such a strong positional advantage that after several hours of fighting the Normans had been all but beaten off. What turned the battle around? William changed tactics. He told his captains to fake a retreat. The effect was to make Harold lose control of his army. Thinking they had won, they abandoned the ridge and ran down the slope in pursuit of the retreating Normans. They fell into a trap. For as soon as they were down on level ground, the Normans turned on them. Stronger and better equipped, the Normans now had the advantage. And they pressed it home.

This is the Enemy's principal tactic: to draw you down from the strategic high ground so he can fight you on the level. While you remain in the heavenly places you have an overwhelming advantage. As soon as you come down to the Enemy's level, the advantage belongs to him. And believe me, he will use it ruthlessly. He will employ any means he can think of to pull you down from the ridge of faithful obedience to God, for as soon as you leave the ridge he can make you forget that he is vulnerable, make you forget that he is a defeated foe. He can neutralize you.

Please concentrate here, because this may be the most crucial point. When it comes to direct combat, the Enemy has three ways of bringing you down. To return to an image I used earlier, he concentrates on three particular doors into your soul. The apostle John outlined them for us in his first epistle:

> *Do not love the world or the things in the world. If any-one loves the world, the love of the Father is not in him. For all that is in the world—the lust of the flesh, the lust*

of the eyes, and the pride of life—is not of the Father but is of the world. (1 John 2:15–16)

The lust of the flesh, the lust of the eyes, the pride of life. These things are of the world, and because they are of the world, they are of the Enemy, who rules this world. Every kind of sin falls into one of these three categories. The lust of the flesh is the craving to satisfy our appetites. The lust of the eyes is the craving for what belongs to others—the sin of covetousness. The pride of life is the decision to step outside of biblical teaching, either to justify our sinful behavior, or—more subtly—to pursue what we think is the will of God. Together these three doors often form a kind of demonic progression. First, we pay attention to the urgings of our fallen nature. Second, we seek to gratify those urges by taking what we should not have. And, third, we seek to render these urges legitimate by rationalizing them and kicking over the traces. As we move along the progression the devil captures, in turn, our passions, our ego, and our will.

You can see exactly this sequence in the story of David's affair with Uriah's wife, Bathsheba. David fell first by submitting to his passions—allowing the sight of Bathsheba to ignite his lust. He fell a second time by coveting her, even though she was another man's wife. He fell a third time, and most seriously, when he tried to disguise her pregnancy by calling Uriah back from the war to sleep with her. By then he was in up to his neck. He wanted Bathsheba so badly he was ready to order her husband's death. One sin paved the way for the next. You can almost see the demons plotting behind the scenes, moving David along, stage by stage, until he was in so deep he couldn't get out. For it is the conquest of your *will* that the Enemy most desires. If he has your will, he has everything he can get—short of your salvation. But more of that in a moment.

First, I want to examine each kind of door by looking at the example of the person who suffered the harshest of temptations and yet held fast. For when Jesus went into the wilderness and was tempted by the devil, it was in exactly these three areas that the devil tempted him: passions, ego, and will.

The Door of the Passions

It is no accident that at the start of his ministry Jesus went into the *wilderness*. He did not go there to get away from it all, as today we might go to a lakeside cabin with a backpack and a fishing rod. He went there deliberately, to face down the Enemy. The wilderness was the place where Satan and his demons congregated. It was their convention center. The Gospel of Matthew tells us very explicitly that "Jesus was led up by the Spirit into the wilderness to be tempted by the devil" (4:1). It was the start of a confrontation with the Enemy that would go all the way to the cross, and beyond—and which would result in the devil being rendered ineffective.

KNOW YOUR REAL ENEMY

(1) So how did Satan begin to tempt Jesus? He began with the passions, the lust of the flesh:

> *And when He had fasted forty days and forty nights, afterward He was hungry. Now when the tempter came to Him, he said, "If You are the Son of God, command that these stones become bread."* (Matt. 4:2–3)

You don't fast for forty days without working up an appetite. The prospect of bread must have been very appealing. As the Son of God, Jesus knew that his food was to do the will of his Father—obedience sustained him. But as the Son of man, he shared the weaknesses and needs of human flesh. When the devil came to him, he was ready to eat.

Notice how subtle the Enemy was. Not for a moment did Satan question Christ's divinity. Rather he treated it as a shared secret. He said, in effect, "Hey, you know and I know that you're God's Son. You could turn that stone into bread with a snap of your fingers, just by saying the word. Why not do it? What's stopping you?" It seemed very reasonable. Jesus needed food. He had the power. God had given him the authority. He could raise the dead, perform healing miracles. Why not do this simple trick of supplying himself with a ready meal? What evil could possibly come of it? Surely this did not even qualify as a temptation—it was simply good sense.

But the evil was real. The issue here was not whether hunger should be satisfied, but whether a fast should be broken. Jesus had accepted the discipline of fasting for forty days. He knew the Father required this of him. To break the fast for the sake of satisfying his hunger, even hours before the allotted time was up, amounted to a serious breach of faith. It would have meant going back on his word. In that sense this first temptation was exactly the same as the temptation to commit adultery. In themselves the appetites aren't wrong—sex and food are both God-given gifts. But both will become evils if indulging them involves breaking a prior commitment. Believers who are married have committed to their spouses, and believers who are single have committed to God: They are not free to indulge their sexual appetites at will.

Similarly, Jesus had made a commitment to the Father to abstain from food for the duration of his stay in the wilderness. He was not free to renegotiate the vow. The invitation to do so implied a challenge to God's authority. When Satan said, "If You are the Son of God . . ." he was suggesting to Jesus that his relationship with the Father was one of complete equality—that he had the right to break his vow if he wished.

Jesus, though, knew the limits of his equality. Though coequal to the Father as part of the Trinity, he was on earth to do his Father's will, not to challenge his authority. Obedience within the Godhead defined Jesus' place at the Father's right hand in glory. Rebellion and self-assertion

could not have made him more "God" than he already was.
He was fully God already. And had he been *less* than God,
rebellion would not have improved his situation—as Satan
well knew.

Many Christians make the mistake of thinking themselves limited by their commitments. They say, in effect, "I
can't do that because God doesn't allow it." But notice how
positively Jesus answered Satan. He did not say "Bread isn't
important, I don't need it," and he did not say, "Fasting is
no fun but I've got to put up with it." Instead he simply put
the appetites in the proper place—*below* the more important business of honoring vows and commitments. He also
made clear that there is much, much more to life than satisfying your appetites:

> *But He answered and said, "It is written, 'Man shall
> not live by bread alone, but by every word that proceeds
> from the mouth of God.'"* (Matt. 4:4)

The secret of Jesus' victory here is the secret of your victory and the secret of my victory. When Satan tries to tempt
you down from the high ground by appealing to your passions, quote him the same Scripture Jesus used. When
Satan comes to you appealing to the flesh, tell him that in
Jesus you have been blessed with every spiritual blessing in
the heavenly places, that in Jesus you have all of your suffi-
ciency, and that you receive more nourishment from obedience to God than you do by indulging your passions.

The Door of the Ego

But Satan will not give up. If he cannot get in the first set of doors, he will try the second. He will move on from the passions to the ego.

He took Jesus into Jerusalem and stood with him on the roof of the temple. That was the highest place in the city— about four hundred feet above the Kidron Valley. From that vantage point the Enemy said to him,

If You are the Son of God, throw Yourself down. (Matt. 4:6)

He was not suggesting suicide. It was a clever tactical switch. Satan had figured out by now that he could not get to Jesus through the passions. Unlike Esau, who sold his birthright to his brother Isaac for a single plate of stew, Jesus would concede nothing even in the grip of a ravenous hunger. Seeing that this door was firmly closed, Satan beat a strategic retreat and rallied to attack on a different front. "Okay," he said, "if I can't get to you through your passions, let me appeal to your ego. You say you believe the Word of God. Fine. Why don't you prove it? Throw yourself down—"

For it is written:
"He shall give His angels charge over you,"
and,
"In their hands they shall bear you up,
Lest you dash your foot against a stone." (Matt. 4:6b)

At first it may be hard to see what Satan hoped to achieve. Throwing yourself off a building is not an idea most of us find attractive. But see Jesus as Satan saw him: a poor man from the country, the son of a carpenter. Without learning, without a track record, and facing a people renowned for their dislike of prophets. To such a man, Satan reasoned, the prospect of beginning his ministry with a showstopping, spectacular stunt must surely seem alluring. And bear in mind that Jesus knew his Father would honor his scriptural promise. If Jesus had jumped, an angelic bodyguard would have flashed out of thin air and saved him. He would have gone from being a nobody to being an instant celebrity.

There is a lesson here. Do not let anyone tell you the devil is ignorant of Scripture. He knows it backward and forward. And he is very adept at producing a verse or two that appear to support his argument. So be wary of people who claim to have unearthed some radical new truth from the pages of the Bible. Look at what they are claiming the Bible says, and which of your instincts they are appealing to. You have heard people on television tell you, "Trust in Jesus and you'll become rich and happy and fat." The fat part may be true—at least it seems to be in my case—but where exactly does Scripture offer these apparently unconditional and cast-iron guarantees? Nowhere. And what motives are the preachers appealing to? Your selflessness and charity? Not likely. Being rich and happy is about as self-centered an ambition as you can have. Note that no mention is made of the cross, of taking up the burden of good works, of sacrifice and martyrdom. Think of those early Christians the Roman emperors fed to the lions. They might have been fat; just possibly they were rich; but happy? Not in the sense today's preachers mean it.

What we are looking at here is the lust of the eye, the gospel of greed. It is Christianity without the cost. All you need to do, it says, is name that promise, whatever it is, and it will be yours. The emphasis is almost entirely on what you *want*. Anything you can see, God will get for you, as if God were Santa Claus. The only input from you is *naming and claiming*—oh, and swallowing whole a completely meaningless version of the Christian faith.

The advertising industry has got this down to a fine art. The advertisers know the connection between *perception* and *desire*. They know that if they display something for long enough and in the right way, you will end up wanting it. You see a fifty-year-old woman on television who looks as if she's twenty—and you want the secret of her looks. You see a famous athlete wearing a particular brand of shoes, and you want those shoes. You see a successful man driving a certain kind of car, and you want that car. You see a person who is skinny as a rake eating low-fat yogurt, and you want that yogurt. All of these images appeal to the lust of the eye. All the advertisers have to do is pick the images they know we like, and attach a product to them. Only occasionally does it backfire, as when a friend of mine told me that cottage cheese is fattening. "Every time I see a fat person," he said, "he's eating cottage cheese."

Do you spend time home shopping via the television? You are being asked to indulge in the lust of the eye. All that matters to the advertiser is that you want the merchandise. He does not care whether you can afford it. He does not care whether you need it. He does not care if you're breaking a biblical principle by buying it. The product is shown to you with the specific aim of making you lust after it. The devil led Eve to do some home shopping when he showed her the tree of the knowledge of good and evil. And what did Eve do? What every home shopper does.

So when the woman saw that the tree was good for food, that it was pleasant to the eyes, and a tree desirable to make one wise, she took of its fruit and ate. (Gen. 3:6a)

Remember how, in Israel's invasion of the promised land, Achan confessed,

When I saw among the spoils a beautiful Babylonian garment, two hundred shekels of silver, and a wedge of gold . . . I coveted them and took them. (Josh. 7:21a)

He succumbed to the lust of the eye. We desire things because we *see* them. We see, and soon we want to do more than just see: We want to *possess.* Ecclesiastes tells us that "the eye is not satisfied with seeing" (1:8), and Proverbs tells us that "the eyes of man are never satisfied" (27:20b).

I remember the story about a spoiled little boy who always got everything he cried for. One day he was crying and crying and crying, because he wanted an expensive vase that was sitting on a shelf, and the housekeeper wouldn't give it to him. The mother came over and said, "Why are you crying?"

He said, "I want that. I want that."

Unwisely—as some parents do, thinking the way to express love for their children is to give them everything they ask for—the mother reached out for that expensive vase and put it in front of the boy. Did he stop crying? No, he cried even louder. His mother came back again and said, "What's wrong now?"

He kept on crying and said, "Oh, I want, I want—I want something I can't have!"

But back to the devil and his temptations. Satan had identified what he thought was a weak point in Jesus. After all, Jesus had come to earth in the form of a man. If he hoped to win anyone over to his cause, he would need to show that he was more than simply human. Why not take the easy route and announce his arrival with splashy headlines? People would join up as though they were going to a circus. Besides which, in order to be born among humankind as Mary's son, Jesus had taken a huge cut in salary and benefits. He must, the devil reasoned, have been missing the glory and worship and unquestioning

obedience of the heavenly realm. If any sin would trip the
Messiah, it was surely the sin of *coveting* fame and success.

Satan was wrong. Without hesitation,

> *Jesus said to him, "It is written again, 'You shall not*
> *tempt the LORD your God.'"* (Matt. 4:7)

Which leaves us with a small problem. Clearly, Christian believers cannot rebuff the Enemy in quite the same
way. We are not God, and Satan is within his rights to
tempt us. We can, however, reject the temptation for the
same *reason* Jesus did. For the fact is, anything Satan can
offer us is already in our possession. Ambition, just like the
appetites of hunger and sexual desire, can be felt in legitimate contexts and for pure motives. And after all, as Paul
wrote to the Ephesians, Jesus

> *made us sit together in the heavenly places in Christ*
> *Jesus, that in the ages to come He might show the exceed-*
> *ing riches of His grace in His kindness toward us in*
> *Christ Jesus.* (Eph. 2:6b–7)

Be careful, then, what you allow your eyes to see and
your heart to desire. For nothing the Enemy offers can
match what you have already been promised in Christ. To
covet—to desire for selfish reasons something that others
possess—is to be drawn down from the heights, made to
fight the Enemy on level ground—and defeated.

The Door of the Will

The lust of the flesh, said John; the lust of the eye; and third, the pride of life. When Jesus would not allow Satan to come through the door of the passions, or through the door of the ego, Satan tried a third entrance: the door of the will.

> *Again, the devil took Him up on an exceedingly high mountain, and showed Him all the kingdoms of the world and their glory. And he said to Him, "All these things I will give You . . ."* (Matt. 4:8–9a)

This was another tactical switch. Jesus had not broken under the pressure of hunger. He had not broken before the lure of instant fame and success. So the devil tied his hanky to a stick and waved it. He made what appeared to be a critical concession.

Look at these verses carefully, because I want to explain something to you. When God the Creator made the world, he handed over the title deed to Adam. He said, "Adam, you're in charge. I'm giving you the scepter." And when Adam disobeyed God and fell for Satan's temptation, his fall sealed a coup. Satan had failed in his bid to take over heaven. But on earth he took command by subterfuge and stealth. He usurped the throne of the universe. That is why the Bible refers to Satan as "the god of this world." He rules it. It belongs to him. His demons have garrisoned the cities of earth and defend their borders.

Why are they doing this? Not simply to impose their rule, but because Satan knows his takeover is going to be challenged. It had always been God's purpose to snatch back the scepter from Satan's hand and give it to Jesus the Christ, the Son of man, who died on the cross and rose again—King of kings and Lord of lords. When the Spirit drove Jesus out into the wilderness, Satan's intelligence networks had given him a pretty good idea of what was going on. They had examined the pages of the Old Testament. They had heard the prophet talking about men and women receiving new hearts, living under a new covenant with God. They knew a second David was coming. They knew the arrival of Jesus heralded the counterattack they had feared for so long. And now here were the two leaders, Jesus and Satan, face-to-face.

Satan offered the hand of friendship. He said, in effect, "All right. I know why you're here. I know you want to win back creation. I also know you are powerful. So why don't we settle this amicably? I'll return to you everything I have taken from God. Everything. It's all yours. I freely sign it over to you."

There is something strangely American about this, isn't there? Can you see it? The attraction of the shortcut. Avoiding the conflict. Avoiding—in Jesus' case—the unpleasantness of crucifixion. The shortcut offers instant gratification, without the cost. Satan was conceding to Jesus his entire program of salvation, his entire mission, victory in the whole cosmic conflict—on the easiest possible terms. See how subtle this approach is. Satan was not asking Jesus to abuse his God-given passions or to covet someone else's property. By giving in to this third temptation Jesus would, on the face of it, have been achieving what God wanted to achieve—the recovery of creation. There seemed to be every reason to say, "Yes, let's go with this."

But read the small print. For Satan attached one simple but devastating condition to his offer:

> *And he said to Him, "All these things I will give You if You will fall down and worship me."* (Matt. 4:9)

In other words, Jesus could have had everything he wanted if only he would *submit his will to the devil.* Probably the devil would have allowed any number of miracles, healings, and good works. He would have permitted fellowship, unity among believers, even the preaching of the gospel—provided the whole enterprise remained under his own control and therefore separated from God. Perhaps, had Jesus given in to this temptation, the church would have looked much the same as it does today. Except that the Enemy would own it, and eternal salvation would be only a mirage.

If the Enemy cannot ensnare you through the lust of the flesh or the lust of the eyes, he will use the pride of life. He will strike the most generous of bargains. He will offer to let you do tremendous good, open up for you a way that seems to fulfill the aims of God's kingdom, asking in return only that you move away from some area of clear biblical truth. We must be wary. Whenever a new strategy or idea is put before us, we must ask: *Will doing this keep me inside the will of God as revealed in the Scripture—or will it move me outside it?*

Let me give you an example from my own church. Many years ago one dear brother was determined to change the way the church was run. He began to organize private meetings and hold behind-the-scenes discussions with some of the members of the leadership group. Around this time I became very ill and was unable to attend church meetings. As soon as I was out of circulation, this brother made his move. He had plenty of attractive arguments for moving the church in the direction he wanted it to go. What he did not say was that the changes he wanted would change the biblical direction of the church. A few members of the leadership group noticed this, but the brother gave them the impression that he had my full approval. Confusion resulted. When I recovered and asked some of my friends how they could have allowed this brother to do what he did, their response was: "We thought you had a reason for it." But I had not even known what was going on. And I certainly would not have permitted the church to shift away from its biblical foundation. Needless to say, when I lovingly confronted the brother afterward, he decided to leave.

There is only one answer to the temptation to step outside the will of God as revealed in God's Word. It is the answer Jesus gave to Satan:

> *Then Jesus said to him, "Away with you, Satan! For it is written, 'You shall worship the LORD your God, and Him only you shall serve.'"* (Matt. 4:10)

STAY WHERE YOU CANNOT BE ATTACKED

Stay at high altitude. Stay on the high ground, where you have power over Satan and are sustained by the Word of God. In close combat, the Enemy seeks first to entice you down to his level, to open up one of the doors you should keep firmly shut. But if you remain spiritually in heavenly places with Christ, Satan cannot—yes, you read it right— Satan *cannot* attack you. You are out of his reach.

When somebody says to me, "I'm under attack," I say, "Let's examine your life. Where are you? Why is the Enemy attacking you? How has he drawn you down?" These are the key questions. Because he could not be attacking you if you had not given him a way in. There is no transferring the blame. You either accept the attack, or you stop the attack and gain the victory when you get back to the high ground where you belong.

Please, please understand that by being attacked I mean in those three areas only: lust of the flesh, lust of the eye, and the pride of life. I don't mean attack in the area of suffering when you are in the very will of God like Job, for example.

There is a world of difference between test and temptation. I will say more about this later on. But here I am strictly speaking of temptation to sin, *not* the suffering for the sake of Christ that every serious believer must experience. In 2 Timothy 3:12 Paul assures us that all who live godly will suffer. This is not what I am talking about here.

Ask yourself what door or doors in your life you are leaving ajar for Satan. What door or doors do you fail to bolt every day? Some Christians think doors only need closing once, and after you have bolted the door you can forget about it and you will automatically have the victory. It's not true. Those doors have a habit of slipping open. Not because God is not faithful to his promises, but because it is up to us to make sure our obedience sticks. Show me a Christian who falls again and again to the same sin, and I will show you a Christian who is not keeping an eye on the doors of his soul.

When I get up at five o'clock and go downstairs to pray, I am already bolting those doors mentally. I still have my eyes closed, I'm hardly awake, but I am imagining in my mind that I am turning the keys in the locks—keeping the Enemy out of my life and out of my family—standing in intercession with the doors bolted. Do that every single day. You cannot afford to be lax. Do you want to be accessible to Satan's emissaries? Do you want to let in the demons that are constantly, whether you know it or not, roaring and prowling, looking for an opening to come in? Unless you deal with your open doors, Satan will steal your peace. Satan will rob you of your joy. Satan will destroy your relationships.

So anytime you feel temptation, ask yourself: *What is this appealing to? To my appetites? To my selfish nature? To my covetous nature? Or to my desire to go my own way instead of God's?* Every temptation falls into one of those three categories. And these are exactly the same categories through which Satan sought access to Jesus' life. Success in any category will please him. But the last one, the capture of your will, is his ultimate prize. He wants us to give in to our appetites so regularly that we begin to rationalize sin as acceptable. To covet something so much that we begin to name that coveting as legitimate ambition. To go about the work of God in ways that put us outside the circle of biblical truth. These things are the Enemy's goal in combat because they drive the deepest wedge between you and your Savior. They put your commitment, your heart, your will, in a place other than God. They feed your self-centeredness and your pride. And they make you repeat the first sin of Adam and Eve—disregarding the word of God and doing what *they* thought was best.

Occupy the high ground. Keep the doors bolted. There is no reason for you to be defeated. Satan may be a seasoned foe, strong and persistent and armed with deadly weapons, but he cannot touch you when you live in obedience to Christ. And—as we will soon see—his days are numbered.

PART THREE

KNOW HOW TO DEFEAT THE ENEMY

CHAPTER 6

K N O W

A

Y O U R

SEVEN-POINT

R E A L

COUNTER-

E N E M Y

OFFENSIVE

HROUGHOUT THIS book I have alluded to some of my own experiences in spiritual warfare. This is one of the hardest things for a pastor and a writer to do—indeed for anyone to do—to take a pair of binoculars and zoom in on his own weaknesses and show how God has dealt with them. It's threatening, but it's also good for me. Because it means I cannot hide behind these pages and pretend I am perfect, or that I have not suffered embarrassing defeats; or that as a minister I am somehow either immune to the kinds of attacks other Christians have to endure or singled out for attacks that are especially vicious. I am, in fact, exactly the same as you: a Christian called to fight against the devil and win.

So what's it like for me?

Let me give you one final example. One area where the Enemy knows he can get to me and rob me of my joy is false accusation. Being in ministry makes you responsible for many small and large decisions; and in all those decisions, the buck stops at your desk. In my case this is made slightly worse by the fact that I have strongly held opinions. As anyone who knows me will testify, my sense of God's calling is very clear. Details often do not bother me. I don't care whether the sanctuary is painted red or white; and it's not an issue who does the job, as long as the job gets done. But when it comes to the direction and the implementation of the ministry vision, I am emphatic.

Now here is the weakness. My shortcoming lies in dealing with the critical attitude of others. If I have reason to suspect that somebody else is critical of me, or of something I think, or of something I have done, I often find my finger on the trigger of a quick reply. Any questioning of my leadership in the important areas of ministry is apt to kindle my anger. I find it difficult to reason with my critics, or to explain quietly why I am taking a particular line, or what circumstances and convictions lie behind my decision. I wish I *could*. I admire the more placid personalities who can reason things out. But that is not my particular character strength. Instead, I am far more likely to stew over some remark a person has made and to spend sleepless nights asking myself useless questions. *Why does this person dislike my preaching style? How could he dare question my passion for evangelism? Doesn't he know me well enough not to question my motives?* And so on.

Let me be even more frank with you. Along the way this tendency has led me into some errors. I have written some harsh letters that I wish I had never written. I have spoken some harsh words that I wish had never left my mouth. Even when I know in my heart of hearts that a rebuke was called for, I sometimes look back and realize that, given the chance again, I would have held my peace a little longer and been more measured in my words when I finally spoke.

Many of you will identify with that. Others will be asking, "Why are you writing a book about overcoming the Enemy if you can't even handle your own problem? Why can't you find a way of dealing with this weakness of yours?"

Well, I have found a way. And I am dealing with it. I deal with it daily, and will continue to deal with it daily until I go to be with the Lord. I fight and, with God's help, win the match round by round—not with a knockout, but on points. I bolt this door of impatience and anger, or any of my other weaknesses, by a seven-pronged plan of defense. This tactic is not composed of quick one-two-three steps; some of them require thoughtful analysis and preparation. You may already know some of these seven points, but you need to remind yourself of these basic defense mechanisms each time the Enemy tempts you.

Number one, I begin by remembering the theme of this book each day: The battle has already been fought, and the victory is ours.

To remind myself that victory is assured, I need look no farther than Scripture or any farther back in the New Testament than the first book, the book of Matthew.

1. REMEMBER: THE VICTORY IS OURS

Even before the Resurrection, Jesus' arrival on earth had started to fray nerves in the Enemy's camp. You can see it in the confrontation Matthew recorded between Jesus and the two demon-possessed men at Gergesenes. These men occupied the tombs. The demons had made these human beings so fierce, people were scared to go near them. Jesus had not been to this place before, and yet—significantly— the demons immediately recognized him and started to talk:

And suddenly they cried out, saying, "What have we to do with You, Jesus, You Son of God? Have You come here to torment us before the time?" (Matt. 8:29)

The word *torment* here means "consign to eternal punishment," something I'll look at further in the final chapter. You can always tell when discipline in an army is about to break down, because the troops stop thinking about victory and start thinking about survival. These demons were doing just that. They recognized Jesus to be their judge. They recognized him as having authority over them. They sensed his power, and suddenly Satan's promises of glory and ascendancy over God looked hollow. It was no longer a question of whether they would be condemned; it was a question of *when.* They saw Jesus and the sulfurous reek of the lake of fire stung their nostrils, and they yelled out, "Have you come before we were expecting you?"

This was panic talking. They did not fight. They did not even threaten Jesus. Uppermost on their minds was saving their own skins. In fact, to keep the eternal flames at bay for a while longer, they were willing to contemplate almost any method of escape:

> *Now a good way off from them there was a herd of many swine feeding. So the demons begged Him, saying, "If You cast us out, permit us to go away into the herd of swine."* (Matt. 8:30–31)

Jesus allowed this, so the confrontation ended with the undignified sight of these one-time angels thundering into the sea inside a herd of pigs. Not the kind of glorious victory Satan envisioned when he made his bid for the throne of heaven!

The story illustrates very well what James meant when he told believers: "Resist the devil and he will flee from you" (James 4:7b). Disarmed, the devil can do nothing to you. It's as if he has broken into your house and found you standing there, pointing a pistol at him. Not only is he helpless, he's scared. When you resist him, he recognizes the presence of Jesus in you—the same Jesus who outwitted him at the cross and who drove his minions into a herd of pigs—and all this once-glorious angelic being wants to do is turn on his heels and run.

Are you this assertive with the devil? If so, why are so many Christians whining and wimping out, instead of facing down the Enemy?

So Why Are We Whining?

It saddens me to say that many Christians never really resist Satan. Instead they go around with bowed shoulders and say, "You know, things are not going well. We've got to watch for this, and we've got to watch for that, and we've got to be careful." They are embattled, penned in, besieged. When they plant churches, they keep away from difficult neighborhoods because the territory is too dangerous. Instead of invading the Enemy's domain, they stay where they feel safe. If they resist the devil at all, they do it so cautiously they might as well keep quiet. They say, "Oh devil, please don't do that. Just stay away from me." And then he comes up and gives them a shiny black eye, and they scurry back to God and say, "Well, Lord, you know I have a weak, fallen nature. I'm trying to resist him the best I can, but I just keep tripping up."

Now let me be straight with you. This is not resisting. This is wimping out spiritually. Did Paul end his letter to the Ephesians by saying: "Finally, my brethren, be wimps in the Lord"? No. He said,

Finally, my brethren, be strong in the Lord and in the power of His might. Put on the whole armor of God, that you may be able to stand against the wiles of the devil. (Eph. 6:10–11)

Nowhere in the New Testament is it suggested that we should be retiring in our attitude toward the devil. Wimps get beaten to a pulp, and they deserve it.

Paul called us to stand in the power of God's might. We cannot forget that Jesus rose victorious from the dead.

But what exactly happened on the cross?

Jesus Frees Us

In one way I hesitate to write about this, because the truth is so glorious it defies our powers of explanation. Though I have been walking with the Lord for over thirty years, I have never ceased to be amazed at the price God paid for my salvation, at what it cost Jesus to mount the counteroffensive into the Enemy's territory. We think God's omnipotence made salvation straightforward, so we end up being blasé about what is the greatest miracle of all time: We have been received back into fellowship with God.

Only in heaven will we even come close to understanding what it cost to make our redemption possible.

Read the words of Paul to the Colossians:

And you, being dead in your trespasses and the uncircumcision of your flesh, He has made alive together with Him, having forgiven you all trespasses, having wiped out the handwriting of requirements that was against us, which was contrary to us. And He has taken it out of the way, having nailed it to the cross. Having disarmed principalities and powers, He made a public spectacle of them, triumphing over them in it. (2:13–15)

The Enemy's greatest weapon against humankind is sin, because by getting us to sin the Enemy draws us down from the heights and defeats us. Yet even in the worst of these skirmishes, he is unable to use his weaponry to full advantage, because Jesus drained sin of its power. He disarmed the Enemy.

To explain how this took place, Paul resorted to a very different image. His talk about nailing handwriting to the cross may seem obscure, but Paul was using language his readers readily understood: the language of the Roman law courts.

The Language of Roman Law

The first stage of a Roman prosecution was for the plaintiff to appear before the judge and present his case. He had to prove his testimony before the accused could even be brought to court. If the case reached the court, the plaintiff was again required to stand up and make his accusation—this time in the presence of the defendant as well as the judge. Paul himself was indicted in this way. In Acts 24 you can read how the high priest Ananias and a hired orator named Tertullus accused Paul before the governor Felix, and how Paul defended himself against the charge. And elsewhere in the New Testament, when Timothy was called on to act as a judge between Christians, Paul advised him not to accept an accusation unless at least two other witnesses substantiated it (1 Tim. 5:19).

In the passage from Colossians, Paul uses the same picture of the Roman legal process to show how Jesus outwitted Satan at the cross. Satan is our accuser. Every day, almost hour by hour, he has been proclaiming the case against us. "Look at Michael Youssef," he says to the Father. "A pastor, and yet he can't turn the other cheek. Such anger!"

And make no mistake—the charges are serious, and the proof plentiful. Satan has done his preparation. He knows the Word of God, and knows the Bible says that the sinning soul shall die. He knows the Bible says that the wages of sin is death. So when Satan, the accuser, comes before God and denounces us for our sins, God, the judge, has to concede that these denunciations are just and true.

None are righteous, says Scripture. Not one. Each of us has sinned and fallen short of the glory of God. The evidence is incontestable. Our spiritual fingerprints are everywhere.

KNOW YOUR REAL ENEMY

We cannot deny the catalog of sins Satan brings against us. He did not have to hire some expensive private eye to go around the country searching and finding evidence. The evidence is staring him in the face!

Long before Satan even began his accusation, in fact, God knew we were guilty. He knew we were born in sin. He knew we would practice sin every day. And God, the judge, could not wink at sin, for he is a fair judge. To be otherwise would be to deny his nature. He could not listen to the accusation against us and then wave his hand and say, "Forget all that, it doesn't matter."

Sin *does* matter. All proved offenses matter. They demand judgment. And God cannot neglect to pass sentence any more than he can fail to determine guilt. Sometimes human courts fail; they condemn the innocent—as in the mockery of a trial that Jesus endured before Pontius Pilate—or they release the guilty. But these things cannot happen in God's court. For God is just. When Satan stands up in heaven and points his finger at you and me, no lawyer in earth or heaven can get us off the hook.

I want to tell you, I have great respect for lawyers; my church is full of them. But God's law does not allow the same kind of disputation that human law allows. There are no extenuating circumstances. There is no possibility of plea bargaining. There are no loopholes or technicalities, no biased jurors. We cannot claim any legal or political immunity. We cannot claim any protection on the basis of our intelligence or social background. We cannot defend ourselves by saying, "Well, you know, I was good here and good here and good here. I was only bad here." In God's law the rule is: One strike and you're out. We were guilty, and—like Satan—we were all going down.

But blessed be his holy name: At that point, Jesus stepped in.

When a criminal was convicted under Roman law and a judge pronounced the sentence, a clerk of the court would be required to write down two things: the offender's crime and his sentence. When the jail guard took the offender to his cell, he nailed the paper bearing these two pieces of information to the door. If he had committed a capital crime—and in the Roman Empire crucifixion was the usual sentence for such a crime—the guard would nail that same piece of paper to the offender's cross. That is why Pontius Pilate wrote a notice on the cross of Jesus Christ: "JESUS OF NAZARETH, THE KING OF THE JEWS" (John 19:19). Jesus was hanging there because he had been found guilty of a capital offense: treason.

But Pilate's sentence was not the only indictment nailed to the cross that day. Go back to Paul's letter to the Colossians. God, wrote Paul,

wiped out the handwriting of requirements that was against us, *which was contrary* to us. *And He has taken it out of the way, having nailed it to the cross.* (2:14, emphasis added)

That *handwriting of requirements* was the indictment of sin against all those God has predestined to know him. It was a record of your iniquity and mine. It was a record of your disobedience and mine.

But it no longer hangs on our cell door. God took it off and nailed it to the cross. Jesus took upon himself the penalty for every sin you and I have committed or ever will commit. He established the bridgehead and opened a way out of Enemy territory. Fully and comprehensively, he silenced every accusation Satan could make about God's elect, and met the requirements of our sentence.

You can see this from the Gospel records of the Crucifixion.

The Last Moment on the Cross

John wrote that at the very end of Jesus' ordeal,

when Jesus had received the sour wine, He said, "It is finished!" And bowing His head, He gave up His spirit. (John 19:30)

The Greek word translated "It is finished!" is *tetelestai.* It is no coincidence that this word also has a legal connotation. Roman law was meant to be scrupulously fair. When a prisoner had served his term in detention, or—as happened occasionally—if he had been pardoned, his jailers would release him and take him back to court, along with the piece of paper that was nailed to his cell door. The prisoner would see the same judge who sentenced him, and that judge would take a pen and write across the page one word: *tetelestai*. Paid in full. The piece of paper that had once bore witness to the bearer's guilt and shame now bore witness to his right to freedom. He had paid his debt. It was finished. Nobody could send him back to prison unless he committed another offense.

Consequently, the freed criminal would often take that piece of paper back home with him and nail it to the front door of his house. If any of his old enemies came by and said, "What is that fellow doing out of prison?" the freed man could point to the piece of paper and to that one word, *tetelestai*. He could say, "You have no claim over me. I am a free man. My debt is paid in full." His safety, his liberty, and his future depended on that one word, *tetelestai*.

And that is exactly the word Jesus used in his last moment on the cross. Notice how Jesus was in control at Calvary. Most people who were nailed to a cross simply hung there and waited to die. Not Jesus.

> *So when Jesus had received the sour wine, He said, "It is finished!" And bowing His head, He gave up His spirit.* (John 19:30)

His life was not taken away from him; he laid it down. And the last thing he did before he allowed his spirit to depart from his body was to utter the cry of victory: *"Tete-lestai!"* Not, "Thank goodness it's over." But, "The price is paid in full, Satan is defeated!"

That, I suspect, was the moment at which Satan first realized he had been outwitted. He had actively pursued the Crucifixion, thinking, perhaps, that killing Jesus would frustrate God's plans. He even entered into the heart of Judas Iscariot in order to make it possible. He did not know that he was playing into God's hands by engineering the death of Jesus, that by inflicting what he thought was a crushing defeat he had unintentionally conceded the decisive battle of the counteroffensive. <u>For that word, *tetelestai,* suddenly and drastically curtailed the Enemy's power</u>. Until that point he had been able to use God's judgment as a weapon. He could say of anyone on earth, "He's mine, she's mine," because God cannot look on the face of sin. But now—to his surprise—there were people over whom he had no power, people whose numbers began growing as the kingdom spread.

The Enemy lost his power. In Paul's words, Jesus "disarmed principalities and powers," and "made a public spectacle of them, triumphing over them in it" (Col. 2:15). If you have committed your life to Jesus Christ, if Jesus is your only Savior and Lord, then Satan has no legal right over you. No legal right to trespass on your property. No legal right to harass you. No legal right to come into your life when he wants to and leave when he wants to. You do not belong to him anymore. When Jesus said, *"Tetelestai!"*

you became a free man, a free woman. At that very instant, locks were installed on the inside of your soul's doors. You could shut the Enemy out. And once those doors have been locked and bolted, there is no reason on earth why you need to have the Enemy trampling over your life and defeating you.

So the first way I bolt the door of impatience and anger is to remember that the battle has been won. I do not have to justify myself. Jesus did it for me. I say to Satan, *"Tetelestai!* It is finished." And I remind myself: "Christ died for you, Michael. Surely you can overcome your anger."

To do that I must also overcome my need to retaliate. And I can only do that if I lay down my life to Jesus in each instance, so that I no longer care what other people think.

2. THE SECRET OF MASADA: LAY DOWN YOUR LIFE

At the southwestern edge of the Dead Sea there is a mountaintop fortress called Masada. The rocky cliffs rise 1,300 feet above the surrounding desert, and on the top of it lie the remains of a military encampment. Masada holds a special place in the memory of the Jewish people, for it was at Masada that Israel's conflict with Rome reached its climax.

In the century after Jesus came, Jewish relations with Rome broke down into a rebellion, which the Romans ruthlessly put down. And the last band of rebels—just 930 men, women, and children—retreated to the rocky peak of Masada.

Standing on top of the towering cliffs, those persecuted people could see the outline of the Roman military camp below. But the rock was almost unscalable, affording the Jewish rebels a secure refuge for several years. Eventually the Romans built a vast dirt ramp—some 200 feet high and 645 feet long—to besiege the stronghold; the remains are still visible today. Once the mighty Roman soldiers finally scaled the walls of the fortress, however, they met no resistance. Every one of the 930 men, women, and children lay dead. They had killed themselves rather than face the indignity of death or enslavement at the hands of the Romans.

So powerful is the memory of that event that every modern Israeli soldier is taken to Masada for a swearing-in ceremony. With history ringing in their ears, they swear never again to let Israel be brought into bondage.

Christians should take note of this. Our invisible war against the Enemy is every bit as serious as the Jewish war against Rome. And like those 930 Jews at Masada, we are called to lay down our lives. I am not advocating suicide (like Jonestown or Heaven's Gate), or martyrdom, or even valor on the field of battle. I simply mean that in spiritual terms we must learn to die to ourselves in order to live in victory, for that is the secret of staying on the high ground where Satan cannot reach us.

Go back to the verse I quoted earlier in this chapter from James. In fact I only gave you the second part of the verse. The full version goes like this:

Therefore submit to God. Resist the devil and he will flee from you. (4:7)

The connection of these two thoughts is no accident. Successful resisting flows from successful submitting. What is most terrifying to the Enemy is the life that is totally dedicated to God in every detail, because this person's heart is ironclad, completely impenetrable to the Enemy's weapons.

Someone asked George Mueller, the great man of faith of the last century (and one of my heroes), "What is the secret of your victorious Christian living?"

Mueller replied, "It was the day I died, utterly died." Then he leaned over, literally touching the ground, as he went on, "Died to George Mueller, to his opinions, to his preferences, to his tastes, to his will. I died to the world, to its approval or censure. Died to the approval or blame even of my brethren and my friends. And since I have done this, I have studied only to show myself approved unto God."

Mueller lived out what Paul the apostle taught in Romans: "For he who has died has been freed from sin" (6:7). Paul went on to explain that a Christian believer has in fact already died with Christ on the cross, so that he now "lives to God" (6:10). The old man has died; the new man has been resurrected. Submitting to God, therefore, can be thought of as keeping the old man dead.

Again, in Paul's words,

> *Do not present your members as instruments of unrigh-teousness to sin, but present yourselves to God as being alive from the dead, and your members as instruments of righteousness to God. For sin shall not have domin-ion over you, for you are not under law but under grace.*
> (Rom. 6:13–14)

We need to surrender in total obedience, without hesi-tation and without reservation. That is the secret of making the devil flee.

When I am falsely accused, I do not need to retaliate even if I am innocent—because I am no longer seeking this person's approval, or anyone else's. I only seek my Father's approval. And I have to tell myself that each time I become angry.

Remember, the battle is ours. Remember the secret of Masada: lay down your life. And third, remember to lock the doors to your soul each morning.

3. LOCK THE DOORS EACH MORNING

I mentioned this previously, but it is so important we need to see it here again as part of our battle plan.

Every morning as I wake up I bolt the doors of my heart that are susceptible to sin. I begin by bolting the gate of the city—every area of my life. The moment I claim I have certain areas of strength—"This area is really fine"—that is the downfall for me. Pride was the devil's sin; it can also be mine.

So I begin by praying for strength in every area: greed, lust, pride. Then I go to the smaller doors, like anger and impatience with people.

The devil cannot defeat us unless we get sloppy and start leaving those doors unlocked. That is the reality for many believers. They are too busy; they miss their quiet time; they get distracted. And sooner or later they discover they have been drawn down from the high places of fellowship with God and are once again taking a knockout from the devil. They feel trapped, as if becoming a Christian has made no difference, as if all their efforts to live a Christian life can achieve no more than a monotonous cycle of failure and guilt. Is that your spiritual reality? If so, take careful note—because Satan has you hoodwinked.

So often, even in the evangelical church, Christians attend worship Sunday by Sunday, listening to the gospel message but going no farther. They get saved on Sunday, but never learn how to live in the power and victory of Christ for the rest of the week. Christ does not lead us in triumphal procession on Sundays only, however. He leads us on Mondays and Tuesdays and Wednesdays and Thursdays and Fridays and Saturdays. Paul pictured us as constantly returning from the war, as the Roman generals did, in a garland-strewn victory parade, marching behind our Leader in his strength.

We are called not only to stop the Enemy from getting into our lives, but actually to drive him away from us. Not only to go around bolting the doors of our soul against Satan, the prowling lion, but to use our own lethal weaponry in such a way that the Enemy flees in terror. And that means that as Christians we have to undergo a training course of the most demanding kind. Let's turn now and look at those next steps—steps that will keep the Enemy on the run.

K   N   O   W

KEEPING

Y   O   U   R

THE ENEMY

R   E   A   L

ON

E   N   E   M   Y

THE RUN

EVERY TIME I preach or write, it is not just a matter of getting up and throwing some Scripture together. My sermons grow out of prayer, and in much of that prayer I find myself on my knees, going hand to hand with the devil.

The next step in my seven-point counteroffensive against the Enemy is what Paul taught in Ephesians 6 about wrestling against principalities and powers. Every soldier needs to put on his battle gear, whether it be khaki fatigues or old-fashioned armor.

4. PUT ON YOUR BATTLE GEAR

I have quoted from Ephesians 6 already, because that is where Paul warned Christians they do not wrestle against flesh and blood, but against the fourfold infernal hierarchy, the Enemy's chain of command. Immediately after Paul's description of the Enemy's forces, he continued with this advice to believers:

> *Therefore take up the whole armor of God, that you may be able to withstand in the evil day, and having done all, to stand.* (v. 13)

Much has been written and preached on the verses that follow. But I believe this armor of God is of three types: the uniform, the defensive weapons, and the offensive weapons.

The Uniform

Paul went on,

> *Stand therefore, having girded your waist with truth, having put on the breastplate of righteousness, and having shod your feet with the preparation of the gospel of peace.* (vv. 14–15)

I don't want to push Paul's analogy too far, but these items constitute a Christian's basic survival kit—the equipment and clothing that identify his necessary attributes and enable him to go where his Commander directs. Jesus' own life was characterized by this same triad: truth, righteousness, and gospel peace. Answering his Jewish critics, Jesus said,

He who speaks from himself seeks his own glory; but He who seeks the glory of the One who sent Him is true, and no unrighteousness is in Him. (John 7:18)

Truth and righteousness belong together. Yet they are not static. They have a purpose, and that purpose, in Jesus, and now in his followers, is proclaiming the gospel.

Look again at that incident where Jesus asked who the disciples thought he was. Peter replied, almost without thinking, "You are the Christ, the Son of the living God" (Matt. 16:16b). Nobody had told him that. As Jesus said, ". . . flesh and blood has not revealed this to you, but My Father who is in heaven" (v. 17b).

At this stage Peter had no idea that truth and righteousness had some other purpose outside of themselves. That was why, not long afterward, he reacted so badly when Jesus shared what he had come to earth to do:

From that time Jesus began to show to His disciples that He must go to Jerusalem, and suffer many things from the elders and chief priests and scribes, and be killed, and be raised the third day. Then Peter took Him aside

and began to rebuke Him, saying, "Far be it from You, Lord; this shall not happen to You!" (Matt. 16:21–22)

Peter disliked change. But that was what the gospel demanded, so Jesus began to break the news. In effect he took the disciples aside and said, "Now, men, I want to tell you something. I'm going to die on the cross, because that's what I have to do in order to redeem you from sin and save you eternally. I'm telling you this now because pretty soon it will be your job to tell the world. Now being true and righteous is one thing. Letting that truth and righteousness spill out in the form of the good news is quite another.

"The first is static and safe. The second puts you out on the open ocean. It is challenging, demanding." And that's when Peter got scared, just as he got scared when he climbed out of the boat to walk on the water with Jesus, and then saw the huge waves below him.

Today's counselors would have treated Peter with kid gloves. They would say, "He needs time to adjust, he needs stress management, he needs therapy." Jesus got right to the core of the issue. He said to Peter,

Get behind Me, Satan! You are an offense to Me, for you are not mindful of the things of God, but the things of men. (Matt. 16:23b)

This was not willfully riding roughshod over Peter's feelings. The preaching of the gospel was just so crucial, nothing but a direct approach would do.

The principle Jesus implied here still stands. Every time you get out of the will of God, you are doing Satan's bidding. There is no territory in the invisible war that is neutral or undisputed. Every area of your life is under the control of either God or the devil. Consequently, even the best reasons for drawing back from God's work are, ultimately, satanically inspired. Every time you let your pride get in the way, every time you shrink back from preaching the gospel and doing what you know God wants you to do, Satan is using you. Every time you refuse to resist the devil, refuse to send him packing, you have bought into Satan's lie. By contrast, however, every time you stand firm in truth and righteousness, you put the Enemy to flight.

Challenges will come every day. When God calls on you to make some really big sacrifice, someone will say, "That doesn't make sense. Don't do it. Let somebody else do it." God calls you to full-time ministry, and others say, "Don't do such a thing. Let others do it." God calls you to take a job that pays less than you think you deserve. You take something below your level, and God says, "Do it because I want to use you in a certain way." And somebody else says, "No, don't do such a thing. Go for the gold."

Sometimes we get it wrong. But, like Peter, we do not have to be burdened by our failures.

KNOW YOUR REAL ENEMY

What do you do when your shoe comes untied? You stoop down and tie it. What do you do if your belt falls loose? You buckle it up again. Similarly, if you're wearing a breastplate, you don't put it down the moment one of the straps falls off. You refasten it. The Christian life is like driving on the highway. If a tire blows, you don't abandon the car. You put on the spare and get back on the road.

One of the reasons Peter is such a great encouragement to me is that he fell so badly, so many times. Yet he never stayed down! He knew how to accept God's forgiveness and start again. So by the time he wrote his epistles, he spoke from a wealth of experience. When I read those words of Peter's I quoted earlier—"Be sober, be vigilant; because your adversary the devil walks about like a roaring lion, seeking whom he may devour"—I know Peter experienced this firsthand.

When Satan tempts me to retaliate, I put on my battle fatigues, my uniform of truth and righteousness. I must turn the other cheek, for the Scripture, God's truth, says so. Then, when I am dressed for combat, I gather together my defensive weapons.

Defensive Weapons

Paul next outlined two pieces of battle gear each soldier must have for protection:

> *above all, taking the shield of faith with which you will be able to quench all the fiery darts of the wicked one. And take the helmet of salvation . . .* (Eph. 6:16–17a)

Do you remember when the people of Israel were living in slavery in Egypt, and Pharaoh refused to let them go— even after nine plagues? Probably the Israelites' confidence in Moses and Aaron hit an all-time low. And yet the next thing they heard from Moses was this:

Pick out and take lambs for yourselves according to your families, and kill the Passover lamb. And you shall take a bunch of hyssop, dip it in the blood that is in the basin, and strike the lintel and the two doorposts with the blood that is in the basin. And none of you shall go out of the door of his house until morning. (Ex. 12:21b–22)

Painting your door with blood did not sound quite as strange to the Israelites as it does to us today. Nevertheless, it must have been tempting to say, "Oh, God, we are suffering here in slavery in Egypt. How is it going to help us to put blood on our doors?"

Or everybody could have gotten together and said, "Let's vote on this." But no—they just obeyed. They did not understand what God had in mind, but they obeyed anyway. They painted blood over the door frames, and went to sleep. In the middle of that night, as God went through the land of Egypt slaying the firstborn, every time he came to a house marked faithfully with the blood, he saw it and passed over that house.

There is a truth in that passage from Exodus, a truth that applies directly to us. Like the Israelites, the only thing separating us from destruction is blood—the blood of Jesus. His blood protects us completely. Once we are marked with the blood we cannot be touched—by God's judgment or by the devil. Because the blood says, "Pass over, do not harm." No power in hell can get past that blood, because it is a seal established on the authority of God and God's Word. God himself has declared that whoever is marked with the blood of Jesus shall stand beyond the reach of the devil. The blood-washed person will be taken into God's territory, into the bridgehead of God's kingdom. The price has been paid for his salvation, that word *tetelestai* striking out the record of his sins.

So remember: You may be assaulted by the Enemy in all kinds of ways. He may come at you through the doors of sin. He may come at you through your emotions. He may come at you through your mental state and feelings of oppression and depression. He may come at you through overwork, stressed relationships, a cooling of your love for Jesus Christ. But whatever route the Enemy takes, no matter how frightening and invincible he looks, the moment you plead the blood of Jesus he will begin to turn and run away from you.

This is not because of anything you are or anything you have done. It does not matter what your net worth is, or what family you come from. It does not matter if you are Episcopalian or Presbyterian or Baptist or Pentecostal. It does not matter how long you have been a Christian. It does not matter whether you find the life of faith easy or hard. Your victory is not based on any of that. Your victory is based on the death and resurrection of the Lord Jesus Christ. His death on the cross not only provided your salvation, but has armed you against the Enemy's onslaught. It is your shield and your helmet.

And this grace of God is given to us day in and day out. It is not something that happened in the past, when you gave your life to Christ and became born again. It is given to you afresh every morning, every hour. God did not call us to hide from the Enemy. God did not call us to outsmart the Enemy by our own resources. No! God called us to plead the blood of his Son, Jesus, to defend ourselves with the helmet of salvation and the shield of faith. He called us to withstand actively, believing the Word of God and what the Word of God says about our authority and victory in Jesus Christ, and about putting the Enemy, the wicked one, to flight.

We have been thoroughly equipped to withstand the Enemy's attack. We have the uniform of truth and righteousness. We have defensive weapons of a shield and a helmet—the blood of Jesus. And we have offensive weapons to put Satan on the run.

Offensive Weapons

Finally Paul says,

And take . . . the sword of the Spirit, which is the word of God. (Eph. 6:17)

KNOW YOUR REAL ENEMY

Jesus used the sword of the Spirit against the Enemy in the wilderness. In reply to the devil's suggestions and insinuations, Jesus simply quoted the eternal, infallible, indisputable, and unambiguous word of God. It works like the ace of trumps. There is no answer to the Word. No way around it, no way beyond it. It marks the end of the argument. It is the *sword* of the Spirit, and that is exactly how you use it—you pick up your sword and go on the offensive. You might make a slight adjustment for the sake of helping your imagination—and that is to bring the technology up to date. Had Paul been writing at the turn of the twenty-first century, perhaps he would have called God's word an Uzi or a semiautomatic.

So how do you use your offensive weapons? Say the Enemy comes to you, through one of his demons or through some other person, and brings doubt to your heart about your Christian walk. He whispers, "Are you really a Christian? Do you really think you are going to heaven?" You pull out the big gun of 1 John 5:11–12, and you say to him: "'And this is the testimony: that God has given us eternal life, and this life is in His Son. He who has the Son has life; he who does not have the Son of God does not have life.'"

Or the Enemy comes to you and whispers, "Your sins are too big for God to forgive. You've done so many miserable things in the past, God could never forgive you." Here's what you do. You pull out 1 John 1:9 and say to him, "'If we confess our sins, He is faithful and just to forgive us our sins and to cleanse us from all unrighteousness.'"

Or the Enemy comes to you and taunts, "Look at your miserable condition! You're not even able to get up from your bed. You can't even shake depression. You're a wreck. How can you say that God loves you?" Here's what you do. You blow him away with Romans 5:8. "But God demonstrates His own love toward us, in that while we were still sinners, Christ died for us."

Or the Enemy comes to you and says, "God doesn't answer prayer these days. If God answered prayer, you'd be out of this mess. Look how long you've been waiting." Here's what you do. You run him through with John 16:24: "Until now you have asked nothing in My name. Ask, and you will receive, that your joy may be full."

Or the Enemy tries to hit you through suffering—physical suffering, financial suffering, whatever trying circumstances you are facing. Throw 2 Corinthians 12:9 at him: "And He [Jesus] said to me, 'My grace is sufficient for you, for My strength is made perfect in weakness.' Therefore most gladly I will rather boast in my infirmities, that the power of Christ may rest upon me."

Or the Enemy says to you, as he does to me, "You've been wronged. You've been falsely accused. You have reason to be angry." Here's what you do. You stab his logic with Proverbs 16:32: "He who is slow to anger is better than the mighty, / And he who rules his spirit than he who takes a city."

When the enemy tries to knock me out, I remember the victory is ours. I remember the secret of Masada: lay down your life. I lock the doors of my soul each morning. I put on my battle gear. And then I begin praising the Lord.

5. PRAISE THE LORD

Several years ago I heard a story about an elderly gentleman who was at a midweek prayer meeting. He began his prayer by saying, "Oh, Lord, we will praise you, we will praise you with an instrument of ten strings!"

People wondered what he meant, until he went on to say, "We will praise you with our two eyes, by looking only to you. We will exalt you with our two ears, by listening only to your voice. We will extol you with our two hands, by working in your service. We will honor you with our two feet, by walking in the way of your statutes. We will magnify you with our tongues, by bearing testimony to your loving kindness. We will worship you with our hearts, by loving only you. We thank you for this instrument, Lord. Keep it in tune. Play upon it as you will, and ring out the melodies of your grace. May its harmonies always express your glory."[1]

Well said, don't you think? You see, praise is total; it is praise of the mind and praise of the heart, as well as praise of the lips.

When you think about it, that's exactly what the angels are doing all the time in heaven. And that's what other

Christians who have gone before us are also doing in heaven. They are continuously worshiping God and praising God and adoring God.

And that is what you and I will be doing when we close our eyes and go home to be in the presence of God.

Now, what does all this have to do with victory over the Enemy?

When I am angry at someone who has falsely accused me, the spiritual realm becomes misty, foggy, unreal. I begin to think that the world I can see is the real world, which is what Madison Avenue and the media are trying to convince me of.

Yet the truth of Scripture is this: What we call "the real world," this tangible world, is not really real. What is real is the invisible realm, the spiritual realm, the realm in the presence of God. And when I praise him, I enter into that heavenly realm.

Praise changes the atmosphere of my anger and bitterness. Praise changes my attitude toward the person who has falsely accused me. Regardless of my circumstances, no matter how difficult they may be, if I begin to praise God I will be uplifted.

Remember that the next time you have an argument with your spouse. Start singing praises, and if you can't sing, get a praise tape for your home and your car. Just praise God.

The devil's hordes are everywhere. When you get out of church, they are sitting in the car, waiting for you, ready to steal your joy and your blessing. That's when the Enemy does his best work, getting people to argue with one another. The way to stop him is to start praising God—and Satan will flee in a minute.

You see, God is specifically present in the praises of his people. And his power is especially manifested in our praises.

Henry W. Frost, a veteran missionary to China, had a great impact on that nation. However, his ministry was not effective until he discovered the incredible lesson of praising God.

In his autobiography he writes, "Nothing so pleases God in connection with our prayer as praise . . . and nothing so blesses the man who prays as the praise which he offers."

Frost then goes on to tell what happened one day when he received sad news from home. "A deep shadow had covered my soul, I prayed and I prayed, but the darkness didn't vanish. I summoned myself to endure, but the darkness only deepened.

"Then I went to an inland station and saw on the wall of the mission home these words: 'Try praising the Lord.' I did, and in a moment every shadow was gone, not to return. Yes, the psalmist was right, it is a good thing to give praise unto the Lord."[2]

In order to praise God properly, we must remember one of the names of God: *El Shaddai,* which was understood by God's people as "God Almighty" or "God of *all power*" or "God who is all sufficient."

El Shaddai means that God intervenes on behalf of his people. *El Shaddai* brought the Israelites out of Egypt.

El Shaddai alone can

- sustain you
- protect you
- redeem you.

El Shaddai will protect me when someone falsely accuses me. As I praise God, I turn the situation over to his power. He has to help me overcome my anger.

And then I begin to pray for the person who has angered me.

6. PRAY FOR
THE
OTHER PERSON

If there is even a grain of truth in what my critic has said about me, I try (I don't need to tell you how hard this is!) to receive it in an attitude of humility. You'll remember that John once responded to Jesus' critics by asking if he should call fire down from heaven to consume them. Most of the time that is very tempting, because it satisfies our craving for revenge.

But that is not what I mean by praying for someone. I mean praying for a person by name. Praying for his business, his wife, and his children. Praying for his well-being. In doing so I find I override my natural instincts. I erase my "default setting" and impose a new behavior on myself. And in my case this is very effective. By doing good to a person who has hurt me, I immediately begin to feel the victory.

Before I mention the final counteroffensive against the Enemy, let's review the first six:

1. Remember: the victory is ours.
2. Remember the secret of Masada: lay down your life.
3. Lock the doors of your soul each morning.
4. Put on your battle gear.
5. Praise the Lord.
6. Pray for the other person.

7. START THINKING
OF
HEAVEN

By this time my critic and I will be in fellowship with each other, and each of us will see the other as God sees us. In other words, I deliberately take myself out of my current time frame. I refuse to see my present situation as enduring or unchangeable. I force myself to look through present imperfection to a future where I am more fully reconciled than I can ever be on earth.

By these means I lock the devil out. I never begin by indulging or even consulting my feelings. I know well enough how I *feel* about a person who has accused me. It's my feelings that are causing the problem. So I move away from my feelings of anger and turn my attention to the eternal truth of God—something stronger than my feelings, and something that is capable of bringing my feelings into line. I know the devil is defeated when I can emerge from this process, meet my critic, and give him a warm—and completely genuine—hug. That does not mean he won't lash out at me again, and that I won't be challenged by my impatience all over again in the future. But that day's battle has been fought, and won.

I think it was Lord Nelson who overwhelmed the French at the Battle of the Nile and then reported the event to the British Admiralty by writing, "Victory is not a large enough word to describe what has taken place in that battle." British understatement, no doubt. But I want to tell you that when you resist the devil, and he flees from you as the Bible promised he would, the whole of heaven is watching and cheering for you. Even in the smallest things, *victory* is not a large enough word to describe what has taken place.

K N O W

THE

Y O U R

ENEMY'S

R E A L

FUTURE

E N E M Y

THE ENEMY is at work everywhere in our culture. And as Christians we find ourselves constantly at war with him. If that is *not* your experience of the Christian life, then something is wrong. Spiritually, you live in a war zone. You cannot be neutral; you cannot avoid taking sides. If you are not fighting with Christ, you are open to the devil. And if you have escaped from the Enemy's clutches and crossed into God's territory, then you are enlisted, and the devil is after you.

Beware of the easy life. Christianity should not be a pleasant cycle of church events: services, Bible studies, coffee mornings, elders' meetings. It's true that if you have closed all the doors of your soul to Satan, you occupy the high ground and he cannot touch you. But if Satan isn't *trying* to attack you, there is something amiss with your Christian walk. You are not stirring him up. You are not making him mad enough. You are not ruffling his feathers. I want to tell you, when I get up in the morning, if I don't have a head-on collision with Satan, I'm worried for the rest of the day. It could mean I'm doing something he likes.

Know your enemy. By now you should know him pretty well. In the past chapters we've looked at every area of his organization and strategy. We have learned about his chain of command. We have learned about his deceptive character. We have discovered how he tries to keep Christians weak. We have found out how he uses the doors of the passions, the ego, and the will to get into your life and manipulate you. We have also learned how Satan was completely defeated at the cross, and how we should apply that victory to our own lives by keeping the devil on the run.

Everyone on the devil's side realizes his time will soon be up, that the invisible war is racing to its conclusion. And so I want to use the final chapter of this book to give you an insight into the Bible's teaching on the future—what the Enemy and his minions' end will be, and what God promises to his soldiers.

SENTENCE PASSED ON SATAN

The Bible teaches us that immediately before the return of Christ there is going to be a tidal wave of rebellion and

sin across the world. It will sweep the entire planet. Why?
Because the devil and his fallen angels know they are about
to be overthrown.

When he died and rose again, Jesus pronounced Satan's
sentence—and he will carry out that sentence when he
returns. Look at John 12, where Jesus was preparing himself for the events that would lead to his death. Two of his
disciples came to Jesus with a request:

> *But Jesus answered them, saying, "The hour has come
> that the Son of Man should be glorified. Most assuredly,
> I say to you, unless a grain of wheat falls into the
> ground and dies, it remains alone; but if it dies, it pro-
> duces much grain.* (vv. 23–24)

Jesus spoke of his death as the hour when "the Son of
Man should be glorified"—not the obvious way to describe
dying. Further, he said that his death would not be the end,
but would result in a greater and glorious multiplication of
life, like the death of a seed of wheat. Shortly afterward he
was even more explicit:

> *Now is the judgment of this world; now the ruler of this
> world will be cast out. And I, if I am lifted up from the
> earth, will draw all peoples to Myself.* (vv. 31–32)

Jesus said, "Satan's rule is about to finish. He thinks that
by crucifying me he will frustrate God's plan for creation,

but the reverse will happen. As I am raised up on the cross, I will draw to myself the whole of humanity." Lord Jesus Christ condemned Satan, and now it is only a matter of time before Christ completes the work he started on the cross. He is going to execute judgment on Satan and all of his demons. Not one of them is going to escape. The power of God will carry them away like flotsam on the incoming tide.

By the end of his earthly ministry, Jesus had already given ample notice of his power over demonic forces. He only had to be in their vicinity to make them tremble. On one occasion, a man implored him to heal his only son:

And as he was still coming, the demon threw [the boy] down and convulsed him. Then Jesus rebuked the unclean spirit, healed the child, and gave him back to his father. (Luke 9:42)

Later Jesus commissioned seventy of his disciples to go out and exercise the same healing ministry. They came back, Luke said, "with joy, saying, 'Lord, even the demons are subject to us in Your name'" (Luke 10:17b). At which point Jesus immediately reminded them that Satan's helplessness in the presence of God is nothing new:

And He said to them, "I saw Satan fall like lightning from heaven. Behold, I give you the authority to trample on serpents and scorpions, and over all the power of the enemy, and nothing shall by any means hurt you. Nevertheless do not rejoice in this, that the spirits are subject to you, but rather rejoice because your names are written in heaven." (Luke 10:18–20)

By the time of the Crucifixion, then, Satan had already been given a foretaste of his final defeat. But it was only a foretaste. In his first coming Jesus bound the demonic powers in just a few cases, by releasing men and women from physical infirmity, by opening the eyes of the blind, the ears of the deaf, and the tongues of the dumb. But in his *second* coming he is going to release *all* of his children from their infirmities. In his first coming those few people Jesus raised from the dead eventually had to die again. But at his *second* coming he is going to raise *all* of his children to live forevermore. In his first coming Jesus delivered as many demon-possessed people as were brought to him. But in his *second* coming he is going to free *all* of his children from satanic oppression and depression.

Again, Jesus gave the clue before his death and resurrection. In the parable of the wheat and the tares, an enemy came and sowed tares—weeds—in a farmer's wheat field. The farmer's servants offered to go and pull them up, but the farmer refused, because in doing so they would almost certainly uproot the wheat seedlings as well. Instead, he said, the servants should wait until both wheat and tares were fully grown, and then harvest the tares first and burn them. In the same way, Jesus explained:

> *The Son of Man will send out His angels, and they will*
> *gather out of His kingdom all things that offend, and*
> *those who practice lawlessness, and will cast them into*
> *the furnace of fire. There will be wailing and gnashing*
> *of teeth. Then the righteous will shine forth as the sun*
> *in the kingdom of their Father.* (Matt. 13:41–43a)

Obviously this is not Satan's favorite Scripture. In fact, in many churches today it's not fashionable to believe in hell—and if you must believe in it, for goodness' sake, don't talk about it!

Why Talk About Hell?

I realize I am on difficult terrain here. The mainline churches stopped believing in hell back yonder when they stopped believing in the Bible. Now many of the popular evangelical churches even refuse to preach on hell. Why? Because, they tell you, hellfire sermons are not seeker-friendly; they are not a good marketing strategy for churches; they do not win friends and influence people.

However, I'm not sure this fear is well founded. Secular universities are now offering courses on hell, and all the press reports I read indicate that students are lining up to take them. If I put on my sociology hat for a moment (I never wear it for long), I suspect this can be explained by the maturing of what is called *Generation X.* According to the people who consider themselves experts in this field,

Generation X covers those born between 1962 and 1982, and has characteristics that differ markedly from the baby boom generation that went before it. Generation X rejects the compromises and hypocrisy of the baby boomers—and praise God for that, because it means they want the truth. Generation X says, "Tell it to me like it is, don't give me the junk." Which could be the reason Generation X may eventually receive the revival America so desperately needs. In fact, the more I read about Generation X, the more it reminds me of days gone by, before your time and before my time ⟨when preachers did not censor their sermons and congregations were strong enough in Christ to take the truth undiluted. ⟩

Be that as it may, hell is still regarded as a taboo subject and, of course, that suits Satan just fine. Satan does not want to hear preachers telling people to get out of Satan's camp and into Jesus' camp. Satan does not want to hear preachers telling people that unless they repent and believe in Jesus Christ, they are going to end up spending eternity there with Satan and all of his demons. Satan does not want to hear preachers warning people to escape from the eternal judgment that is coming upon the world. Satan does not want to hear preachers talking about the lake of fire prepared for him and his angels. So soft-pedaling the truth about all these things, as the mainline churches are doing, fits Satan's plans to a tee. He is not upset when people laugh at the idea of fire and brimstone and a personal devil. When people trivialize hell and treat it as a joke, the Enemy is delighted. The fewer people who take hell seriously, the more companions Satan is likely to have.

So I've got to tell you, as much as it grieves me to disturb anyone's sleep, I can preach nothing more and nothing less than the truth of the Scripture. Am I trying to scare you into heaven? Yes, I am. I have absolutely no hesitation in scaring the socks off you, as long as that will bring you into God's kingdom. After all, unlike a blockbuster horror movie, hell is *real.* You *ought* to be scared—unless, of course, you are on God's side already, in which case death and hell will hold no terrors for you.

The great revivalist Peter Cartwright was warned as he entered church one Sunday morning, "Mr. Cartwright, whatever you do, be very careful of what you say. President Andrew Jackson is going to be in the service today."

Cartwright said, "Fine." He got up to preach, and said, "I am told that President Andrew Jackson is in the congregation. Well, let me tell you before I preach that President Andrew Jackson is going to hell if he does not believe in Jesus Christ."

People were aghast. They were horrified. They didn't know where to look. And after the service most of them left the building with their chins in the air. But not the president. Andrew Jackson walked up to Cartwright, shook his hand warmly, and said, "Sir, I want to tell you this morning that if I had a hundred men like you in my regiment, I could take on the world."

So what does the Bible tell us about hell?

Hell in the Bible

The Bible contains several snapshots of hell. One of them comes in Jesus' parable of the sheep and the goats. Remember that the sheep were distinguished from the goats on the basis of the way they treated "the least of these My brethren" (Matt. 25:40). As Jesus explained, the sheep on the King's right hand were the righteous, accepted into eternal life for ministering to the sick, the stranger, and the prisoner. By contrast, the goats assembled on the King's left hand made the mistake of doing exactly the opposite. Said Jesus:

> *Then He will also say to those on the left hand, "Depart from Me, you cursed, into the everlasting fire prepared for the devil and his angels."* (Matt. 25:41)

The same picture of hell—as a place of everlasting fire—can be found in the parable of the rich man and Lazarus, and also in Revelation. But Matthew's picture of the sheep and the goats tells us something important. Although unbelievers will end up in the lake of fire, the lake of fire was *not made for them.* It was made for Satan and his angels, and existed long before the creation of Adam. Even now it is waiting. John describes the upcoming event through eyes of faith, which are able to see the future as a present reality:

> *The devil, who deceived them, was cast into the lake of fire and brimstone where the beast and the false prophet*

are. And they will be tormented day and night forever and ever. (Rev. 20:10)

Notice something else. The Bible makes it clear that hell is a literal place. It is not a state of mind, not a figment of the imagination, not a literary device. No—hell is a real place, just like Washington, D.C., or Paris, or Honolulu) To read the text in any other way is to indulge in wishful thinking. Jesus was also explicit about the intense suffering of those who are going to be there. He emphasized that there is no return from hell, and that it imposes eternal separation from loved ones—eternal separation, in fact, from all that is good and holy, including God himself. Jesus talked about these things not because he delighted in them, but because he was warning us. Knowing that hell exists, and knowing what hell is like, is something that helps us not to end up going there. The last thing God wants is for anyone else to follow Satan into everlasting punishment.

But if hell is a literal place, is it also *literally* an eternally burning lake? Twenty-one places in the Bible, all in the New Testament, refer to hell as a place of unquenched fire. Some people consider that the only truth worth having is literal truth, and insist that if the Bible talks about hell as a lake of fire, then it must be exactly that. In response their critics have pointed out that, since the earth, and indeed the universe, contains a finite quantity of combustible material, sooner or later a literal hell would run out of fuel. Some of them have even tried to calculate how many millions of years will elapse before this happens. If hell can only burn as long as its fires can be fed, they argue, it is not, strictly speaking, *eternal.*

In my view this whole argument is a waste of time. The Bible is full of expressions God does not expect us to take literally. To pick an example at random, it would be doing a disservice to the Scriptures to insist that the "woman clothed with the sun" in Revelation 12:1 is literally wearing the sun like a pair of jeans. That is not how John meant us to understand him. In this and many other instances, the Bible is using a figure of speech to illustrate a principle, and there are two things we need to remember about this use of figurative language and symbols.

First, symbols in the Bible are not meant to blur an issue or diminish its importance. That a passage or a phrase is symbolic does not make it any less true. It simply alerts us to the fact that some spiritual realities cannot be described directly or by literal means, because the truth lies so far beyond our ordinary experience that using symbols or figures of speech is the only way of helping our finite minds to grasp it.

Second, it is important to remember that the thing being symbolized is always greater than the symbol. Let me give you an example. Every Sunday morning at my church we have a Communion table bearing some bread and some wine. We say that the bread represents the body of the Lord Jesus Christ. It is not *in fact* the body of the Lord Jesus Christ, because the body of the Lord Jesus Christ is in heaven. He is already there at the right hand of the Father. But the bread serves to remind us of the body of Christ. God is accommodating to our finite minds. This is exactly what is happening in Revelation when we read about streets of gold and gates studded with precious stones. Is God putting a commercial value on heaven? Not at all. He is finding things in our own world that will help us visualize things in a world we have never seen.

In the same way, the phrase *lake of fire* is not meant to be taken at face value. Hell is something other than a literal lake of fire, and actually something much worse. Were we able to take a photograph of hell, it might not look at all like a lake or like fire—nevertheless *lake of fire* is the term in our language that conveys more accurately than any other how it feels to be there.

Fire is not the only idea the Bible uses to describe hell.

The Anatomy of Hell

Four more symbols show us what kind of place hell is, and what a terrible fate it is to be trapped inside it:

(1) **Confinement.** The parable of the unforgiving servant (Matt. 18:21–35) pictures hell as a prison. But hell is not like a physical prison. Earthly prisons confine the body, but not the soul or the mind. Earthly prisons cannot chain down the spirit. No matter what happens to the body, the spirit is free to worship, free to create, free to imagine, free

to anticipate, free to hope. When Paul and Silas were beaten up and thrown into the Philippian jail, they were suffering some of the worst privations a human prison has to offer. Nevertheless they were singing and praising God. Physical confinement could not repress their joy in the Lord.

Similarly, Western hostages taken during the 1980s in Beirut survived by nurturing an inner freedom to match and combat the claustrophobic conditions in which they were kept, in some cases for years on end. Jesus' words in Matthew—"Do not fear those who kill the body but cannot kill the soul" (10:28a)—might serve as a hostage's motto.

But there is a second and more chilling part to Jesus' saying: ". . . rather fear Him who is able to destroy both soul and body in hell" (10:28b). Hell locks up not only flesh and blood, but imagination, thought, creativity, hope. And it does so permanently. Prisoners in Venice were once housed in a building accessed by a single bridge over a canal. The bridge, which still stands, is called the Bridge of Sighs—for no prisoner going across it ever crossed back the other way. Hell keeps its victims, and it makes Alcatraz look like a Scout camp!

(2) Darkness. John said in Revelation that the new City of God will need no created light because Jesus himself will illuminate it. Jesus is the light of the world. In contrast, hell is portrayed as a place of perpetual blackness. "Cast him into outer darkness," the king ordered his servants in the

parable of the wedding feast—thus consigning the man who had stolen into the celebration to hell (Matt. 22:13). Similarly, in the parable of the talents, the king ordered, "Cast the unprofitable servant into the outer darkness" (Matt. 25:30a). In one way this darkness is literal, for hell has no morning or evening, no twilights or glorious sunsets. But the darkness is also moral and spiritual. The intruder to the wedding feast and the unprofitable servant are both *excluded* from the places where they had once belonged. Hell is a place where things *do not* happen, a place of benightedness, dullness, and ignorance. There is no light for reading, but there is also no newspaper to read, no news at all.

(3) Suffering. In the outer darkness encountered by the wedding intruder and the unprofitable servant there were "wailing and gnashing of teeth." Hell is a place of terrible suffering, a place of constant agony. There is no relief, not for one second. Jesus told the story of the rich man and the beggar Lazarus, whose fortunes were reversed after death so that Lazarus was carried by angels to Abraham's bosom while the rich man roasted in hell.

And being in torments in Hades . . . he cried and said, "Father Abraham, have mercy on me, and send Lazarus that he may dip the tip of his finger in water and cool my tongue; for I am tormented in this flame."
(Luke 16:23a–24)

(4) Loneliness. It is often said that people who go to hell will at least be in good company. George Bernard Shaw once commented that all of the interesting people will be in hell. (The apostle John gives a short list of these interesting people in Revelation: "the cowardly, unbelieving, abominable, murderers, sexually immoral, sorcerers, idolaters, and all liars" (21:8).) They shall all, added John, "have their part in the lake which burns with fire and brimstone." Well, I would not invite these people to *my* birthday party. In fact, it is unlikely that in hell you would enjoy the company even of this dubious crew. For there is no fellowship in hell. One of its characteristics is the absolute isolation of each individual. C. S. Lewis once said there are no personal relationships in hell. It is solitary confinement. Once there, all feelings of attachment, of friendship, and of love, will be forgotten forever.

With stakes this high, it is no wonder we are fighting in the invisible war. But there is coming a day when we will fight no more battles.

LOOKING AHEAD

We need to know our Enemy—to understand him, to outmaneuver him, to keep out of his reach, and to drive him away. But at the same time we should not get our priorities out of order. We should not pay Satan the compliment of thinking about him so much that he comes to dominate our lives. We need to be sober and vigilant. Yet we also need to be oriented to the positive. We need to keep our eyes on Jesus, the author and finisher of our faith. For the closer we are to him, and the more we appreciate and come to value the good things of God's kingdom, the more natural it will be for us to reject the devil's temptations and to live in the Spirit.

One of my friends and church members died recently. He knew he was about to die, and in the last weeks of his life he dedicated himself to telling as many people as he could about heaven. Right to the end, he looked forward. He said, "I've been religious all my life, but on March 28, 1995, Jesus came into my life for the first time." He told all his friends. He told all his family. It was so exciting to see somebody looking forward to heaven. He had the right perspective. In the end, you can't compare the thrill of heaven with the horrors of hell; however, whatever else you can say about the Enemy, he is certainly a bore.

So what reward does God have for those who fight in his army? Just what is it like in heaven, where God's people will reign once the battle is over?

THE PROMISE OF HEAVEN

Some say that heaven is just a state of mind, often the same people who tell us the same lie about hell. Heaven, they say, is an abstract idea. Wishful thinking. A figure of speech.

To those pessimistic people I want to say, loud and clear, that heaven is a real place. In John 14 Jesus said so. He uses the Greek word *topos*, which means exactly that. A place. A location. Jesus told his disciples in this chapter of the Bible, "I go to prepare a place for you" (v. 2b).

And Jesus is not the only one who saw heaven as a place, although that would have been sufficient for me. Just before he was martyred, Stephen, the first deacon of the church, said, "Look! I see the heavens opened and the Son of Man standing at the right hand of God!" (Acts 7:56).

And John, the apostle God chose to give a brief glimpse into eternity, said, "I looked, and there before me was a door standing open in heaven" (Rev. 4:1a NIV).

No abstract idea. No figure of speech. Heaven is a real place with real people who have real bodies. Real life and real joy. Real peace. There are even real angels there.

And that is where my real home is. In fact, all the soldiers in God's army are going there.

The Bible gives us six descriptions of our life in heaven:

1. We Shall Have Uninterrupted Fellowship with God

Someone once asked D. L. Moody, "What are you expecting to do when you get to heaven?"

"I expect to spend the first thousand years looking at Jesus," he replied.

I am not excited by the pearly gates and the streets of gold, whatever they are. Like Moody, I am excited about spending years just looking at Jesus. The apostle Paul knew that this would happen: "For now we see in a mirror, dimly, but then face to face" (1 Cor. 13:12a).

I will see my Lord face-to-face! And so will you.

After Jesus told his disciples he was going to prepare a place for them, he promised them,

> *And if I go and prepare a place for you, I will come again and receive you to Myself; that where I am, there you may be also.* (John 14:3)

Heaven would not be heaven without Jesus and without the ability to fellowship with him forever.

Heaven is a real place—a place of rest.

2. We Shall Rest from the Battle

In describing his vision of heaven John said,

> *Then I heard a voice from heaven saying to me, "Write: 'Blessed are the dead who die in the Lord from now on'* . . . *that they may rest from their labors, and their works follow them."* (Rev. 14:13)

Some people think this means that we are going to be idle in heaven. That may be the vision of the Great Society, but that was not John's vision. He did not see us lying on fluffy clouds and strumming harps. Far from it!

Yet we will rest from the spiritual battle against Satan and the world. We will no longer have to fight temptations and the devil. We will not have to struggle constantly to keep the world from squeezing us into its mold.

The rest in heaven is similar to the Bible's concept of the Sabbath. Unfortunately this earthly day of rest is one of the most misunderstood commandments. The Sabbath was not created to play golf or tennis or to go to the beach. (I don't mean to step on any toes here, but that's just not the biblical concept.)

God set aside the Sabbath so we can take our minds off the mundane and humdrum activity of our lives—in order to focus on him. It is to be a Sabbath unto the Lord.

Remember what Jesus told the Pharisees when they were so concerned that he had healed on the Sabbath. Healing, they said, was work, and work was forbidden on the Sabbath. Jesus tried to explain to them that the Sabbath was made for man, not man for the Sabbath.

The Sabbath is set aside because God knows we will otherwise get busy and work hard—and leave God out. So the Sabbath is a day we focus on God for twenty-four hours out of the week. We focus only on God—his holiness, his majesty, his dominion, his power, his mercy, his grace.

And when the Bible talks about rest in eternity, that is exactly what we will do. We will go from the secular to the sacred, from the humdrum to the holy, from the mundane to the majestic—not just one day a week, but all the time.

Heaven is a real place, a place of rest, and a place where we will serve our Lord.

3. We Will Serve the Lord

John also said about heaven,

And there shall be no more curse, but the throne of God and of the Lamb shall be in it, and His servants shall serve Him. (Rev. 22:3)

The Greek word translated "serve" here, *latreuo,* indicates that there will be joyful service, enthusiastic service, voluntary service to the Lord God. Whatever the service, it will not be a chore. It will not be accompanied by fatigue. Our service will come from our gratitude to God for redeeming us, for getting us into heaven in the first place.

The Bible gives an indication that this service includes reigning and ruling with God. Have you thought about this?

In Matthew 25 the master told the faithful laborer:

Well done, good and faithful servant; you have been faithful over a few things, I will make you ruler over many things. (v. 23)

Whether I receive one dollar or ten trillion dollars to manage in this life does not make any difference, because

God owns it all. What does matter is how faithful I have been with what God has given me.

And what about you? Will the Lord say these words to you: "Well done, good and faithful servant, you have been faithful over a few things, I will make you ruler over many things"?

Heaven is a real place, a place of rest, a place of service, and a place where we will know and understand all things.

4. We Will Have Full Knowledge

After Paul told the Corinthian Christians, "For now we see in a mirror, dimly, but then face to face," he added, "Now I know in part, but then I shall know just as I also am known" (1 Cor. 13:12).

How often we hear questions like, "Why does God allow bad things to happen to good people?"

On earth I don't know why diseases, war, and suffering occur. In heaven I shall understand it all.

Here I don't know why earthquakes and hurricanes happen. But there I shall understand it all.

I shall see things so clearly from God's perspective, there will be no need even to ask questions.

And I don't believe for a moment that anyone will be able to say, "God, you did not give me a fair chance"—especially those who rejected him.

A real place, a place of rest, a place of service, a place where we will know all, and a place of continuous glory.

By beholding we become changed!

5. We Will Be in a Place of Continuous Glory

If you do not spend time looking to heaven now, something is wrong with your faith. You are not living the victorious life, the life Paul described to the Corinthians.

The apostle Paul did not teach God's Word in an air-conditioned sanctuary. In Ephesus, for instance, he could only rent a hall when the philosophers were not using it, and they had all the halls reserved during the morning and evening, the cool of the day. So Paul could only teach in the middle of the day, in the sweltering heat, at a time when everybody else was resting.

Several times soldiers lashed Paul on his back. People stoned him. The Romans persecuted him, as did the Jews. Some Christians who could not forget how he had persecuted them before his conversion on the road to Damascus even hated him. In all of this, he focused on heaven so he could withstand the pressures of earth:

> *For our light affliction, which is but for a moment, is working for us a far more exceeding and eternal weight of glory.* (2 Cor. 4:17)

The word *glory* in this passage refers to the revelation of the character of God in Jesus Christ. In heaven God's character will be so revealed in us, we will be transformed to be like him. The apostle Paul told the Colossian Christians:

When Christ who is our life appears, then you also will appear with Him in glory. (3:4)

And, finally, heaven is a place where we will be in constant worship.

6. We Will Be in Constant Worship

Please, whenever you think of worship in heaven, do not be tempted to equate it with the average 11:00 Sunday morning worship service.

I was once told about one of the most prominent citizens of England, who confessed to Lord Riddle, "When I was a young man, the thought of heaven was more frightening to me than the thought of hell. . . .

"I pictured heaven as a place where time would be perpetual Sundays, with perpetual 11 A.M. service from which there would be no escape. It was a horrible nightmare that made me an atheist for ten years."

Instead of the average Sunday morning service, think of worship as I described it in Chapter 6. The book of Revelation also gives us a picture of the exuberance and excitement and unspeakable joy of worship in heaven. John said,

I heard a loud voice of a great multitude in heaven, saying, "Alleluia! Salvation and glory and honor and power belong to the Lord our God!" (19:1)

I can only imagine the sound and sight of all believers of all ages—Old Testament saints, New Testament saints, saints from all the ages—together with the myriad of angels and musicians, all worshiping the Lord, who is right there in the center of them. Imagine the shouts of hallelujah and the amens punctuating the crescendo of heavenly singers and the fanfare of celestial trumpets.

C. S. Lewis said of heaven, "All the things that have ever deeply possessed your soul have been but hints of it—tantalizing glimpses, promises never quite fulfilled, echoes that died away just as they caught your ear. But if it should really become manifest—if there ever came an echo that did not die away but swelled into the sound itself—you would know it. Beyond all possibility of doubt you would say, 'Here at last is the thing I was made for.'"[1]

I look forward to seeing you there. Keep up the faith!

NOTES

CHAPTER 7
1. Info Search computer software, No. 1493.
2. Ibid., No. 1563.

CHAPTER 8
1. C. S. Lewis, *The Problem of Pain* (New York: MacMillan, 1962).

ABOUT THE AUTHOR

Michael Youssef, Ph.D., was born in the Middle East. He is uniquely gifted in making the Scripture and Bible culture, the culture of his origin, come alive and be relevant to the modern Western world. He is the founding pastor of The Church of The Apostles, an evangelical church in Atlanta, Georgia. He completed his theological training in Australia and received his master's from Fuller Seminary and his doctorate from Emory University. He is internationally known as a trainer of evangelical leaders, having consulted with and served as the managing director of the Haggai Institute for Advanced Leadership Training.

He is the president and host teacher of a national radio ministry, Leading the Way International. He is heard on hundreds of stations around the world. His previous books include *The Leadership Style of Jesus* and *America, Oil, and the Islamic Mind.*